RICHARD A. ISAY, M.D.
Becoming Gay

Richard A. Isay, M.D., is currently Clinical Professor of Psychiatry at Weill Cornell Medical College and in private practice in New York City. He has served as chairman of the Committee on Gay and Lesbian Issues of the American Psychiatric Association, as vice president of the National Lesbian and Gay Health Association, and on the Board of Hetrick Martin Institute for Gay and Lesbian Youth in New York. Dr. Isay is the author of two other books: *Being Homosexual: Gay Men and Their Development* and *Commitment and Healing: Gay Men and the Need for Romantic Love.*

ALSO BY RICHARD A. ISAY, M.D.

Being Homosexual: Gay Men and Their Development

Commitment and Healing: Gay Men and the Need for Romantic Love

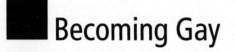

Becoming Gay

The Journey to Self-Acceptance

RICHARD A. ISAY, M.D.

VINTAGE BOOKS

A Division of Random House, Inc.

New York

FIRST VINTAGE BOOKS EDITION, MAY 2009

Grateful acknowledgment is made to Yale University Press for permission to reprint "The Gay Therapist" by Richard Isay from *The Psychoanalytic Study of the Child*, Vol. 46 (1991), edited by A. Solnit. Copyright © 1991 by Yale University Press. Reprinted by permission of Yale University Press.

The Library of Congress has cataloged the Pantheon edition as follows:
Isay, Richard A.
Becoming gay : the journey to self acceptance / Richard A. Isay
New York: Pantheon Books, © 1996.
p. cm.
Includes bibliographical references and index.
1. Gay men—United States—Psychology. 2. Gay men—Mental health—United States. 3. Psychoanalysis and homosexuality—United States. 4. Self acceptance. I. Title.
HQ76.2U5183 1997
155.3—dc21
95026209

Vintage ISBN: 978-0-307-38977-0

Author photograph © Gordon Harrell

www.vintagebooks.com

Printed in the United States of America
10 9 8 7 6 5 4 3 2 1

For Gordon Harrell

The courage to be is the courage to accept oneself as accepted in spite of being unacceptable.

—PAUL TILLICH

Contents

Acknowledgments

I am grateful for the opportunities I have been given to discuss portions of this book at grand rounds in the departments of psychiatry at numerous medical centers throughout the country, at meetings of several psychoanalytic societies, on symposia at annual meetings of the American Psychiatric Association, and at meetings of the National Lesbian and Gay Health Association. Particularly gratifying have been invitations to speak to student groups: the NYU School of Social Work Gay and Lesbian Alliance; LAMDA Health Alliance of Columbia University's Health Science Campus; the Gay, Lesbian and Bisexual Student Association of Harvard Medical School; and the Gay and Lesbian Association of Cornell University Medical College.

I feel privileged to have been asked to give plenary presentations at the Institute of Human Identity in New York City; at a meeting of Integrity at the General Convention of the Episcopal Church in Indianapolis; at the Southern Conference on Lesbian, Gay, Bisexual and Transsexual Health Issues in Tampa; and at an annual meeting of the American Association of Physicians for Human Rights in New York. And I had an opportunity to discuss several chapters early on at an all-day conference sponsored by the Washington State Society for Clinical Social Work in Seattle.

Gordon Harrell has given me the time to write and the constancy, love, affection, and forbearance that have enabled me to do so. I remain grateful for all this and much more.

Finally, I want to express my appreciation to my patients, whose willingness to confront themselves has made both the book and genuine dialogue possible.

Preface

Self-esteem is enhanced by being out. The sense of inauthenticity that inevitably results from remaining closeted leads to injurious inhibitions, making it difficult or impossible to find happiness in the love of another. It is essential for a gay man to oppose antihomosexual bias wherever he finds it, not only to change this prejudice but to dissipate his anger. To be compliant with the homophobia of any organizations or institutions where we work or affiliate is debilitating and antithetical to developing a positive, loving self-image.

There is now greater acceptance of homosexuals and gay relationships than in 1996 when *Becoming Gay* was first published. Currently two states, Massachusetts and Connecticut, have legalized same-sex marriage, and several other states recognize civil unions or partnership that give gay couples nearly all of the same legal rights and responsibilities as heterosexuals. Such social change, along with education and advocacy for gay rights in some schools, has made it easier for adolescents to acknowledge their sexuality to themselves and their peers, and to seek out other gay youth for friendship and romance. And there are now far fewer therapists who believe that sexual orientation is mutable and that gay adolescents who are in conflict about their sexuality should attempt to become heterosexual.

The chapter on HIV/AIDS was written when treatment was neither as effective nor as available as it is today. Although many of my healthy gay patients were having difficulty forming and sustaining their relationships, I found that those who were HIV-infected were turning for the first time to the love of another for comfort, and that these relationships flourished during the course of their illness. The quest for love seems to thrive when there is a sense that life is transient. Now that AIDS is usually a treatable chronic disease because of early diagnosis and new therapies, young gay adults are once again practicing unsafe sex. The rate of infection in this group is rising, and young gay men are not as readily turning to the love of another for their comfort and security as they did when AIDS was usually fatal.

Society's gradually increasing tolerance has made it less uncomfortable for gay men to come out to their family, friends, and at work. But I still see many who are in unhappy heterosexual marriages. Injured self-esteem makes it difficult for them to acknowledge their sexual orientation and too ready to accommodate familial and social pressure to live conventional heterosexual lives. At the same time, I am seeing more middle-aged and older gay men than I did ten or twenty years ago who, emboldened by the recognition of same-sex relationships, are attempting to establish or sustain a committed relationship.

I continue to believe, as I suggest at the conclusion of this book, that loving another and being loved is the most effective means for a gay man to create positive self-regard in our society. But committed love is still difficult for some and will remain so until continuing social change makes it possible for the parents of homosexual children to provide them with the love, empathy, and understanding that every person needs.[1]

---

[1]See my book, *Commitment and Healing: Gay Men and the Need for Romantic Love* (Hoboken, NJ: John Wiley & Sons, 2006).

Becoming Gay

Introduction: Being Homosexual and Becoming Gay

Throughout most of my forty-year career as a psychoanalyst and psychotherapist, traditional Freudian psychoanalysis provided the most widely accepted view of the origin and nature of male homosexuality. The theory holds that a man desires someone of the same sex because a binding, engulfing mother kept him from being close to and thereby identifying with his father, or because a father, emotionally distant or physically absent, caused his child to turn to the mother and identify with her. In both scenarios the male child was feminized by identifying with his mother instead of his father, and, at about age five or six, at the time of the oedipal crisis, he deviated from normal heterosexuality and was on the perverted path of desiring other men instead of women.

As late as the mid-1980s, there had been only minor changes in the psychoanalytic view of male homosexuality.[1] Although it was no longer true, as it had been only a decade earlier, that analysts were equating the quality of homosexual relationships with those of schizophrenics,[2] or stating that homosexuals are "predatory . . . and do not make good citizens, in any society,"[3] most psychoanalysts and analytically oriented psychotherapists still held tenaciously to the idea that normal development led only to heterosexuality and that the same early parental failures that had caused homosexuality also produced severe personality disorders in all homosexuals. This theory contributed to the self-loathing of many gay men.

I have had the unique opportunity of spending the first half of my career seeing heterosexual men and the latter half, homosexual men. Starting in 1980 I began to work with gay men as patients who had no interest in changing their sexual orientation. They came with problems in living, working, and relationships that were similar to those of my heterosexual patients in the years before. Their histories, along with studies suggesting that the concordance of homosexuality is higher in monozygotic twins than in dizygotic twins and non twin siblings, convinced me that homosexuality in men was constitutional and probably genetically determined.[4] This conclusion contradicted the prevailing psychoanalytic view that homosexuality was caused by a disturbed early relationship with parents.

I had found that, like the population of heterosexual men who recalled opposite-sex attraction from an early age, many homosexual men could remember experiencing same-sex attraction when they were as young as four, five, or six years. For gay men, this earliest attraction is to the father or father surrogate. It is often repressed and, like the heterosexual's early attraction to his mother, is recollected with difficulty or in a distorted form, displaced onto another male such as an older brother, relative, or family friend. Just as most clinicians generally assumed that the early appearance of opposite-sex attraction suggested a biological predisposition to heterosexuality, I assumed the same to be true for the same-sex attraction of homosexual men.

The same-sex fantasies and erotic desire of homosexual men, like the opposite-sex fantasies of the heterosexual men I had worked with, were usually stable and persevered throughout their lives, also suggesting a biological rather than familial basis for their sexual orientation.

Gay men usually remembered that they had felt different as children of four, five, or six years, a difference sometimes recalled solely in terms of such early behavior as greater sensitivity, more highly developed aesthetic interests, or a lack of interest in rough-and-tumble activities. But they also eventually recalled their different sexual attraction. The recollection of being atypical boys, while real for most, was often also unconsciously used as a screen memory that kept them from remembering an early attraction to their father.

I observed no difference in the parenting of my heterosexual and homosexual patients that could account for their homosexuality. I had worked with heterosexual men who had distant fathers and engulfing mothers, and was seeing homosexual men who had loving and average-expectable parents. However, the father of a homosexual son may withdraw from him because of the discomfort caused by his child's affection and attraction or by the feminine or gender-atypical manner or behavior characteristic of many of these boys.[5] The less masculine the boy appears, the more likely the father is to withdraw or to reject him in favor of another sibling. The result is an early assault on the self-regard and sense of emotional well-being of many homosexual children, reinforced by later peer rejection, prejudice, and hatred, which may cause significant emotional damage and affect the nature and quality of their adult relationships.

Another observation also suggested to me that homosexuality was biological and not environmentally induced: serious psychological damage may be caused by therapists' attempts to change their patients' homosexual behavior to heterosexual or simply to inhibit their homosexual impulses. Although psychological distress may, of course, be caused by efforts to change any behavior that is fixed, whether it is fixed by very early environmental determinants or by its being constitutional, it was the severity of the depression and anxiety caused by these attempts of former therapists that further suggested the biological basis of my patients' sexual orientation.[6]

On the basis of my clinical observations, including the inhibiting effect of society and psychological conflict on homosexual behavior, I suggested in *Being Homosexual* that homosexuality not be defined by behavior but by the predominant erotic attraction to others of the same sex since childhood. One need not engage in sexual activity to be homosexual, any more than one need engage in sexual activity to be considered heterosexual. In fact, to be homosexual one need not even be aware of sexual fantasies, which may be repressed by conflict and the internalization of social bias. Same-sex fantasies should become available to these individuals during a properly conducted analysis or therapy.

Because my clinical experience and personal observation have, by and large, been with homosexual men, in this book, as in *Being Homosexual,* I am addressing their developmental issues only. In my previous book I used the terms "homosexual" and "gay" synonymously because I was attempting to move my analytic colleagues from the medical model of homosexuality as pathology and deviation to a position that was more humanistic, scientific, and clinically useful. But in *Becoming Gay* I attempt to use "gay" to designate one who is aware of being homosexual and who then develops a personal identity as a homosexual man. Although clinical observation and empirical studies suggest that we are born homosexual, my work with gay men has made it clear that we learn to be gay. The manner as well as the comfort with which one expresses sexual impulses, or even whether they are expressed at all, seems to be determined by social and cultural mores as well as by our earliest experiences and relationships.

In our culture, for example, in spite of a lack of heterosexual desire, many male adolescents who are homosexual will date girls or attempt to have sex with them because of parental, peer, and social expectations. On the other hand, in ancient Greece it was a matter of social status for a heterosexual man of good birth to have an adolescent male lover, as long as the older man was the pursuer and the active partner in sex. It was also an honor for the youth to be loved and desired by one with status and power, and it was viewed as a gift from the youth to the elder for the former eventually to accept his sexual entreaties.[7]

In a modern but distant and foreign culture, adolescents of Sambia in New Guinea are inseminated by elders as part of their initiation rites into manhood. Probably some of the youthful partners in Sambia, as in ancient Greece, have an innate disposition that is homosexual, as do some of the adults who engage in these homosexual acts, but most of the adult males live with women and, like their youthful partners, are constitutionally heterosexual.[8]

To become gay one must be able to label oneself as "homosexual" or "gay." Homosexual boys who have loving parents who acknowledge and accept their different sexual feelings and their different kind of maleness will usually grow up having strong, positive self-regard. They will also be more likely to label themselves "gay" with greater comfort and possibly even at an earlier age than those who feel they must conform to society's expectations in order to be loved. Those whose parents have rejected them because of their homosexuality will generally, as adults, be self-deprecating and angry and, therefore, much less capable than those who have felt accepted and loved by their parents of engaging in mutually loving adult relationships.

Awareness of sexual orientation is enhanced in early adolescence by pleasurable homoerotic fantasies and later homosexual experiences. Satisfying sexual experiences motivate the adolescent or young adult who has a healthy self-image to come out to other gay peers and adults and then to parents and close family members, consolidating his identity as a gay person.[9]

It is healthy for an adult to come out in all areas of his life, including to important straight people, in order to provide continuity between his internal, private life and his external, social life. Coming out alleviates the anxiety and depression caused by the sense of inauthenticity that arises from hiding or disguising oneself. Closeted gay men are usually cautious and circumspect in their social discourse and relationships. After coming out, they inevitably affirm that they are now more self-assured and that all relationships, including those with straight people, are more authentic and, therefore, more gratifying.

In a society that is prejudiced against homosexuals, a gay man's active opposition to discrimination is important for solidifying his social identity and to feeling positively about it. It is usually a manifestation of poor self-regard for a gay man to participate in institutions, organizations, or professions that discriminate against homosexuals without contesting their bias, no matter how out he is in other areas of his life.[10] The anger that is evoked by prejudice, unless one turns it outward to combat the bias, will inevitably be directed against oneself in masochistic enactments, depression, or further self-esteem injury.

But it is the affirming love of another man that is the most effective antidote to the battered self-esteem of most gay men in our society. And it is the love of another over time that provides the greatest certainty and clarity about one's personal identity as a gay man. Only then does being gay become indispensable to one's happiness.

Becoming Gay is about my patients' experiences learning to be gay at different stages in their lives. It is also about my own experience becoming gay and how my early development and the later course of my personal and professional life made this journey painful and, at times, hazardous.

Although this book is not about doing therapy, I hope it will help clinicians identify those aspects of the lives of their homosexual patients that may have kept them from affirming themselves and feeling positively about their gay identity. And I hope that *Becoming Gay* will deepen the understanding gay men have of themselves and their development.

1

Becoming Gay:
A Personal Odyssey

*We seek other conditions because we know not how to enjoy our own;
and to go outside of ourselves for want of knowing what it is like inside
of us.*

—MONTAIGNE

In Yale's psychiatry department during the 1960s, most of us studying to become psychiatrists believed that psychoanalysis was the optimal therapy for emotional disorders. The analyst, with his esoteric technique that included a couch, free association, and four or five sessions a week over at least that many years, appeared to have greater access to the hidden recesses of his own mind, as well as to the mind of others, than did the psychiatrist in his face-to-face, once- or twice-weekly therapy. Psychoanalysis also offered an all-encompassing theory of mental functioning and human development, and reading Freud was not only intellectually engaging but great fun. The majority of psychiatric residents at that time wanted to be analyzed; many of us hoped to become analysts.

I had wanted to be a psychoanalyst since my third year at Haverford College. In a course on nineteenth-century philosophy I had read Schopenhauer and Nietzsche, whose views about irrational sources of human behavior and the unconscious mind intrigued me. Jung's speculative thinking about myths, archetypes, and archetypal images provided a bridge between my interest in philosophy and a growing fascination with academic psychology. I had no idea that my burgeoning interest in the mind was due to distress and confusion over a longstanding attraction to other boys.

In my freshman year I had fallen in love with one of my classmates. I first saw Bob on the train returning to college from Thanksgiving vacation. He had a slender, well-proportioned, athletic body, dark hair, which he wore in a neat brush cut, soft but intelligent brown eyes, and a warm, engaging smile. I thought he was incredibly handsome. I admired how comfortable he was with our classmates and how much they, in turn, appeared to want him to like them. Although too shy to speak to him on the train, I noted his every move and developed a crush and the determination to get to know him. We lived near each other in the same dormitory, and with a studied nonchalance that belied my excitement I'd drop over to his room to chat. We gradually became friends and decided to live together the following year. I moved into the suite he was sharing with two roommates.

In my sophomore year a recent graduate of Harvard's clinical psychology program had joined Haverford's faculty to teach psychology. He was a demanding and dynamic teacher, interested in psychoanalytic theory and the contributions psychoanalysis had made to understanding human motivation and behavior. In his course on personality we read Freud's views on homosexuality as a perversion, and I became convinced that I was sick. But from what I learned the next semester about adolescence in his course on human development, I comforted myself with the knowledge that some attraction to other boys was natural and that my infatuation with Bob was a passing phase that would soon be replaced by an equally passionate interest in girls.

Since I was never attracted to girls, I dated infrequently. My evenings and weekends were spent studying, often simply to avoid the appearance of having time on my hands. My roommates were all diligent students. Bob was pre-med and worked hard, although his considerable academic achievements often appeared effortless. Another roommate, Jack, was the college German scholar, who immersed himself in German literature in addition to his premedical studies. Their dedication to academic pursuits, along with my own, usually made it unnecessary for me to date except on rare occasions such as the annual college dance, when I felt social pressure to do so.

I looked forward to the time that Bob and I spent alone and was jealous when he was with other friends, particularly his girlfriend. I fantasized about spending the rest of my life with him, longed to have unlimited access to him and the time and freedom to touch and be close to him forever. I knew that I had fallen in love, but I believed it was due to his being a kind and thoughtful person. The idea that my desire was the passionate expression of a sexual orientation never crossed my mind. Although Bob and I engaged in casual sexual play, I did not label myself "homosexual." I did view my attraction to him as a serious neurotic problem since I was uncertain that I fell into the category of those normal adolescents who simply had occasional thoughts about other boys.

Midway in my third year of college I was concerned enough

about my attachment to Bob to attempt to speak about it with my psychology professor. On the way to his office I recalled his response to a student who had asked him how to distinguish between an eighteen- or nineteen-year-old who had normal homosexual thoughts from someone who was actually homosexual. "You might worry," he had said, "if you see a soldier in uniform, he looks attractive, and you wonder what his body looks like." By the time I had arrived at the office door, convinced that he would think I was homosexual even though I was unable to, I decided not to mention being in love and, instead, spoke with him about my career indecision. I thought I detected some incredulity when he asked me if anything else was troubling me, and I uncomfortably responded, "No."

In fact, I was concerned about my future career plans. By the second semester of that junior year I had decided to go to graduate school in clinical psychology in order to become a psychoanalyst, a decision that I knew was partly motivated by concern over my own emotional distress and the belief that I could benefit from treatment. But in the spring of that year, as president of the Haverford–Bryn Mawr Psychology Club, I had the opportunity to spend time with the famous psychoanalyst Erich Fromm, who had been invited to lecture at the college. He was accompanied by his blond and attractive second wife, who seemed quite a bit younger than he. I was impressed by how adoring they were of each other, and though it was clear he would have preferred being alone with his new wife, I took every opportunity to talk with him about the future direction of my career. Fromm had studied sociology and political science before psychoanalysis, but he advised me to go to medical school and become a psychiatrist before receiving psychoanalytic training, assuring me that psychiatry offered more career opportunities and financial security than psychology did at the time.

By the end of my junior year I had decided to follow his advice, and I began to take the necessary and arduous premedical courses the following year. Neither my senior year of college, in which I began my premedical studies, the postgraduate year in which I completed them, nor my first two years of medical school studying the preclinical sciences held much academic interest. These courses, however, kept me preoccupied and depressed. I was both too busy to date women and too distressed to be aware of my homosexual desire.

Bob told me in the spring of our last year of college that he planned to marry immediately after graduation. Jealous and angry, I tearfully opposed his marriage and told him so. He listened patiently, but seemed relieved that I would be traveling during the summer and unable to attend his wedding. When I visited him on occasional weekends the following years in Boston, where he was in medical school, I was consumed by anguish and jealousy whenever he and his wife would retire to their bedroom. Depression over my separation from him contributed to my lack of interest in sex during this period.

I was aware that I had homosexual masturbation fantasies and was occasionally conscious of longing for sexual contact with men, but I continued to believe that my desires were symptoms of emotional difficulties that could eventually be cured. I had read enough psychoanalysis to be convinced, as analysts then believed, that if I was not having sex, I was not really homosexual. Also, at the time I was convinced that in order to be accepted for training as a psychiatrist or as a psychoanalyst I would have to be heterosexual, so in my second year of medical school I set out with determination to date women.

The summer before my third year I met my future wife. We went out several times that summer while I was in New York City on a fellowship and she was home from college. I thought it was a sign of the severity of my emotional problems that I was not attracted to women, and my lack of passion made me more eager than ever to begin treatment. With the help of an analyst, and providing I did not give in to my homosexual impulses, I believed that I would be able to put such feelings out of my mind and eventually be able to marry.

I did not contact her for another three years. Although exhaustion during my internship year in Cleveland had extinguished most of my social inclinations and much of my sexual desire, I did notice my attraction to some of the men I shared on-call rooms with. I became eager to start treatment the following year to rid myself of these unwanted impulses.

Two months after beginning my training in psychiatry at Yale, I started to look for an analyst. I spoke with two. Both were certified to analyze candidates in psychoanalytic training, so I assumed that they would be knowledgeable and clinically proficient. The first was the chairman of the Education Committee of the Western New England Institute for Psychoanalysis in New Haven. When I called to speak with him, his secretary told me that I could make an appointment only by writing and describing the nature of the difficulties for which I felt I needed to be treated. Since he was educational director of the institute, I thought he would be the best analyst. I should take note, I believed, of his request to put my problems in writing, since this must have important technical significance. Several years later he told me that he was somewhat phobic and avoided speaking on the telephone except when doing so was unavoidable.

During the consultation he asked me about my sexual experiences with girls. I had no difficulty telling him that I had none since he, overweight, quite bald, and shy, gave the impression that he was asexual. However, even he seemed a bit surprised by my sexual inexperience and inactivity.

I told him about getting turned on by wrestling with my friend Lou in his attic on weekends in high school and the mild sexual activity at college with Bob, but I did not think to tell him I had been in love, since he seemed to be interested only in my sexual behavior and not in my longing for love from a man. Nor did he inquire about my homosexual masturbation fantasies. He was reassured by my relative lack of homosexual experience and by the fact that I was once again trying to date. At that time I shared his conviction that homosexuality was simply a matter of sex, not of love, and that if I did not act out my desire then I was emotionally disturbed, but not homosexual, and could become heterosexual.

I liked this man because of his lack of pretension and his emotional responsiveness. I felt strangely comforted by his obvious eccentricities. I was flattered that he offered to take me on as a patient, but he could see me only once a week until he had more time available to begin an analysis the following year. Believing I could be cured only if I saw someone daily, I decided to look for another analyst.

Ruben Samuels was by reputation a nice guy. He was in his mid-fifties and was also designated by the American Psychoanalytic Association to train future analysts. He seemed to be kind, intelligent, and patient, although somewhat depressed. He was encouraged that I had not had sex with a man since college and was clearly enthusiastic about my continuing to date. He seemed very normal. I had even heard that he swam regularly at the Jewish community center, which, since I had never been athletic, gave me an added sense that, unlike myself, he was a thoroughly heterosexual person. Although his apparent normality made me feel uneasy, I decided to start analysis as soon as he had an opening, which would be a few months from our first consultation. I had found an analyst like the father I would have wanted.

My father had died suddenly of a myocardial infarction three days after my twelfth birthday. He had left college during his first year to work, and, although warmer and certainly kinder than my mother, he also lacked her education and cultural interests. His friends seemed, like him, to be inclined to sports and little interested in intellectual pursuits. I was shy, withdrawn, awkward, and unathletic. I've always believed that I disappointed him by not being masculine enough.

My analyst appeared to be kind and masculine like my father, but he also had the intellectual curiosity and culture that my father had seemed to lack. And since we shared an enthusiasm for psychoanalysis, I believed I had a chance to redo the relationship with my father.

Although I was a good psychiatry resident and enjoyed my work, I felt lonely, depressed, and, at times, desperate. I thought that my despair was the result of an inability to express my inhibited heterosexuality; I never imagined that it could be the result of the denial and suppression of my homosexuality. I had recognized by then how strong my homosexual feelings were and, most likely, knew unconsciously the futility of attempting to arouse the "blighted germs" of my purported heterosexuality; however, since I thought of myself as being emotionally disturbed and not gay, I had never contemplated finding sexual and emotional gratification with another man.

I had liked my future wife from the time we met. I knew she had the qualities of character and intelligence of someone I could marry. But I had not contacted her until one month before my consultation with Dr. Samuels. I desperately wanted to please him and tried to do so by anticipating his wish that I give up my homosexual desire by dating and having sex with girls.

I had been waiting for about eight years to begin treatment; the four months between consulting with my future analyst and starting the analysis felt endless. On the day we finally began, Dr. Samuels explained the basic rules of saying whatever came to my mind. I lay down on the couch and wept about my loneliness and inability to experience any passion. After a few days, we decided that analysis six times a week rather than the usual four or five seemed indicated because of the severity of my heterosexual inhibition and considerable unhappiness.

Like all analysts at the time, he advocated and promoted my own conviction that sexual attraction to men was a serious emotional affliction. He implied that by becoming aware of the childhood fear of my father's rage over my closeness to my mother I would become less frightened of the mortal consequences of my heterosexual desire, heterosexuality would flower, and homosexual desire would subside.

In the second year of analysis I had sex with a woman for the first time, but I was persistently anxious about losing my erection, which happened with discomforting frequency. Sex was neither passionate nor fun. In that same year, for a brief time, I developed a distressing symptom of genital anesthesia, a symptom that Dr. Samuels interpreted as a symbolic autocastration that expressed my anxiety about becoming increasingly heterosexual. His interpretation of the childhood terror of my father's retaliation had little effect on my impotence. Only after I had completed analysis did I understand that the genital numbness had been another way of trying to please my analyst, since it kept me from masturbating and having the homosexual fantasies that were tellingly present whenever I did.

In my third year of analysis my future wife and I became engaged. My analyst, who had never called me by name in our sessions because he felt it would interfere with the perception of his neutrality, enthusiastically congratulated me. And although he was on vacation at the time, he sent a warm telegram to the synagogue on the occasion of our marriage the following summer.

During the early years, frequent impotence became persistent whenever Ruben went on vacation, a symptom that he interpreted again and again as being caused by fear of my heterosexuality and the repressed anxiety, grief, and anger over the untimely death of my father at the onset of my adolescence. It was not until I had finished analysis that I understood that what episodic heterosexual behavior I had been capable of had been motivated by my desire to please my analyst, and when he went on vacation my heterosexuality did as well.

The denial of my homosexuality had always been strong, and now the daily contact with my analyst, who usually implicitly but sometimes explicitly conveyed his view that I was a neurotically inhibited heterosexual, provided me with little opportunity to consider the idea that I was homosexual.

Furthermore, my desire to be a psychoanalyst was contributing to the denial of my homosexuality. Analysts assumed that the same early trauma that caused one to become homosexual produced such severe personality defects that analysts who themselves were homosexual would be unable to sustain the emotional constraint, neutrality, attentiveness, and empathy that enable one to do competent therapy. Therefore, persons who were actively homosexual were not accepted for training at psychoanalytic institutes affiliated with the American Psychoanalytic Association. Since I was making an effort to rid myself of homosexual fantasies and to disinhibit my heterosexuality, I believed I could be accepted and decided to apply for psychoanalytic training.

Three senior analysts interviewed me. Although I was cautiously truthful about my sexual history, the Education Committee undoubtedly saw my eagerness to spend one hour every day labeling myself neurotic as a sign of emotional health. Furthermore, it seemed impossible for psychoanalytic educators, as it had been for my analyst, to reconcile the reputation I had as a psychiatry resident who had done good clinical work with patients with the idea that I could be homosexual. I did not look or act like all homosexuals were assumed to appear or behave—effeminate, odd, or in some other way unconventional. It was for these reasons, I believe, and because I was not acting out my sexual fantasies, that the Education Committee did not consider me to be homosexual and I was accepted for training.

I continued my analysis with Dr. Samuels. My self-image and self-esteem did improve somewhat as a result of the recollection of troublesome aspects of my childhood that had been repressed. My depression, however, did not improve, due to the difficulty I now experienced having any sexual feelings or impulses whatsoever. I also had a problem thinking clearly around my analyst. He believed all these symptoms were caused by anxiety about showing him my masculine aggressiveness because I feared him as I had feared my father. But the aggressiveness I was anxious about had nothing to do with masculinity, as he had suggested; it was caused by a need to inhibit my mounting anger with him. I was devoting most of my psychic energy to repressing my sexuality and anger and was consequently becoming more depressed. I was getting worse, not better.

I was the middle of three children, placed between an athletically inclined older brother, who I felt was preferred by both my parents, and a sister three years younger who was clearly adored because of her cute, winning ways. I was awkward, shy, and overweight, and when my sister was born, I believed, as do many children, that my parents were eager to have her so they could get rid of me. She was the object of much attention, and the more attention she got, the more obstreperous I became.

One of the early memories recollected in my analysis was from soon after my sister's birth, when, feeling neglected by my mother, I refused to leave her to go to bed. Frustrated, she tied me with rope to the mattress and locked my door. Out of terror and fury I struggled to get out of bed, pulling the mattress on top of me, falling asleep exhausted, trying to find air.

Neither of my parents was affectionate, either with each other or with their children. I grew up believing both that expressions of affection were unnatural and that sexual excitement was inappropriate. My father was chronically unhappy and depressed. He often spent entire weekends in bed; we saw little of him and our care was left to my mother. Although she was more tolerant of my lack of athletic prowess and of my aesthetic interests than he, my mother was also swifter to anger. She had felt emotionally deprived by her own parents, particularly by her domineering mother, and she had little patience for the emotional needs of her children. She demanded obedience, and punishment was swift and severe.

Like many homosexual boys, I felt I had been a disappointment to my father. I went to camp to please him, starting at age seven, until the summer after his death, when, at age twelve, relieved, I did not have to return.

The last three years had been particularly difficult. I was then at an athletic camp; we went relentlessly every day from softball to tennis and, with terror, once a week, to boxing. I did enjoy swimming, which was a respite from the demands to compete athletically because I could float for long periods of time. I also enjoyed the changing room and showers, where I watched other boys with a curiosity and enthusiasm that was lacking at other times in my day.

It was a month after returning home from camp and a few days after receiving a report from the director that my father asked me to go for a ride with him and a friend. I was excited to be with him, seated in the front seat between him and an obviously powerfully built man. He asked me to feel his friend's large muscular arms. "That," he said, "is how I want you to look." I was deeply embarrassed. I was sure his heart had been chilled by the report that I was uncoordinated, immature, and the "outstanding homesick boy of the season." He died six months later, at age forty-five, of a heart attack.

Soon after his death my mother began to comment about my being overweight, awkward, too shy, and unathletic. I imagine she feared that a sensitive, shy adolescent who shunned competitive sports and lacked a masculine presence might become homosexual. She asked the family pediatrician to talk to me about sex. After a thorough physical exam, he lectured me about the relationship between healthy exercise and a clean mind. He assured me that exercise would also make me look "more like a boy." He suggested that I do situps and cautioned me about masturbating, which I had not yet attempted, but which, soon thereafter, I successfully tried.

My masturbation must have come to my mother's attention, since a friend of my father's came over to our house one evening soon after I had discovered how to do it to tell me not to and to warn that it could interfere with my liking girls. While not deterring me, these talks did make me wary of having any erotic thoughts. They also contributed to my growing conviction that sexual excitement was not only inappropriate but bad and harmful. While in analysis I grew to believe that my parents' inability to express affection and to convey a sense of their own sexuality, along with the discouragement of my sexuality as an adolescent, had all contributed to the inhibition of my adult heterosexual desire. After my analysis, I understood that my belief that all sex was bad helped to explain why I had persistently denied my homosexuality and why I thought it to be a sickness.

Recollection of childhood memories, some of which had been repressed, was helpful in improving my sense of self-worth, but my analyst's conviction that homosexual impulses were simply a defense against my latent heterosexuality made me feel more defective because I could no longer experience any passion. Although increasingly hopeless, I continued to obey his implicit admonitions not to act out homosexual impulses, which we both understood could cause my dismissal from the psychoanalytic training program or, at least, an interruption until such behavior ceased.

Analysts at most institutes were required to report their patients' progress to the Education Committee in order for a candidate to progress to didactic courses and to treat patients under supervision. The implicit power held by one's training analyst, no matter how well intentioned or protective of confidentiality he was, could at times inhibit any analysand's behavior, thoughts, and fantasies. Because I did trust my analyst's discretion and believed that the reporting requirements at my institute were minimal and would not require violations of confidentiality, I was not conscious of concerns that my behavior or homosexual impulses would hinder the progression of my career. Nevertheless, unconscious fear of being reported undoubtedly added to the difficulties I continued to have in acknowledging to myself that I was homosexual.

In the fall of 1971 my analyst raised the question of terminating treatment. I had been seeing him for nearly ten years and, for seven of these years, six times a week; for three years, five times weekly. He felt we had done as much work as possible.

I was now rarely functioning sexually, and when I did it was with great effort. I had rationalized that maturity and mental health demanded the sublimation of sexual excitement in work and in responsibility for the welfare of others. I was also relieved by the idea of stopping. It meant that I had my analyst's approval and would soon graduate from the institute, the first of my class of candidates to do so. The date my analyst and I had set for the actual termination was about eight months from that time, which gave us an opportunity to deal with old conflicts and transference issues that would manifest themselves in the face of terminating.

On at least two occasions during that last year I browsed gay pornography in New Haven bookstores. My analyst and I concurred that I was attempting to sabotage my career as well as my marriage and that this behavior was motivated by anger at him for stopping treatment. He reminded me that I had felt both abandoned and relieved when my father had died, believing that these old feelings were being revived in the transference.

His observations were partly correct. However, neither of us then understood that the prospect of terminating and of not having to comply in the future with his expectations of heterosexuality was enabling me to feel somewhat more comfortable expressing my homosexual desire and inclinations.

When I finished my analysis, I was in my mid-thirties and had a wife and two children, all of whom I loved. By then I had stopped having sex because I no longer felt a need to please my analyst by continuing to try. My unsuccessful efforts had caused me more anguish than pleasure, so I was relieved. But I was a caring husband and father, felt guilty about depriving my wife of sex, and viewed my lack of heterosexual passion as a serious deficiency.

Childhood rivalries with my brother and sister, the longing for the love of both my parents, and the pain and anger I experienced from feeling unappreciated by them no longer affected my current relationships as they had before my analysis. I was now better equipped to recognize these old feelings when they reemerged with my wife, children, colleagues, patients, and friends. I had discovered new ways of dealing with them that were no longer so self-defeating, spiteful, or defensive. But because of my analyst's heterosexual bias, I was further from understanding at the end of analysis than at the start that my lack of heterosexual desire was due to my being homosexual.

An analyst or therapist who sees his patient four or five or, as in my case, six times a week induces a passivity that encourages in most an acquiescence, compliance, and responsiveness to his views no matter how indirectly suggestions are made or how careful he is to attempt to remain neutral. I had been told repeatedly that my homosexual impulses were but ways of inhibiting my heterosexuality and, since I wanted to believe it, had unquestioningly accepted my analyst's perception that I was an impaired heterosexual.[1]

Shortly after we stopped, I began to experience and express more anger and to think about why I had had trouble with these emotions during my treatment. The problem had been caused partly by the difficulty my analyst had allowing me to be angry with him. In my consultation he had set forth the rule that I was not to consider him late until he was more than five minutes late. Our hours frequently did not start on time, but if he was ten minutes late and I complained, he would wonder why I was so angry since, according to our agreement, he was only five minutes late. If he was less than five minutes late and I complained, then he insisted I must be displacing my anger about someone or something else onto him since he was not to be considered late at all until after five minutes. His logic consistently enraged me, but I learned to suppress my anger, understanding that he did not like confrontation and had difficulty being seen as flawed.

After terminating the analysis, I also thought about the death of my father, recalling that at my birthday dinner I had attempted to make a declaration of rights for twelve-year-olds, which included the right to smoke. He disagreed and I argued and, being unable to impose my will, furiously left the table. His sudden death a few days later, along with my mother's physical punishments, had convinced me that disagreement with authority in the pursuit of my own conviction would always have disastrous consequences—another reason I had a problem expressing anger while I was in treatment.

It was only three or four months after stopping analysis that I again began to have vivid homosexual fantasies, impulses, and dreams. It was then I recognized that I had been denying and repressing homosexual feelings because I had longed for my analyst's approval and that one way to please him had been to comply with his conviction that I was not homosexual. I knew my need for his approval had been an unanalyzed aspect of the transference, inadvertently used by him in his attempt to make me heterosexual.

Finished with my analysis, I no longer felt passive and compliant and was more comfortable with my anger. I also had less need for social approbation, having learned in my analysis how this need had been caused by feeling unloved as a child. Furthermore, the love I got from my wife and children, along with my professional success, had enhanced my self-confidence.

Six months after completing treatment, while in New York at the fall meeting of the American Psychoanalytic Association, I went to a gay pornographic movie. Within a few minutes, because of the intensity of my sexual feelings, I realized that, in fact, I was homosexual. For the first time, because my sexual feelings and impulses were so clear and powerful, I did not believe I was sick. I experienced a sense of relief and exhilaration. I knew that homosexuality was the passion I had believed myself incapable of ever experiencing.

For the next weeks elation alternated with intense and utter despair. I was devoted to my wife and two children and was nearing completion of training in a profession that was prejudiced against and intolerant of homosexuals. I was excited by the prospect of expressing my sexual passion, but I could not conceive how the confines of my life would ever permit this.

Closeted because of my marriage and my profession and terrified of being discovered, I was able to express my sexuality only in anonymous encounters. One convenient place to have sex was a rest stop on the Connecticut Thruway near New Haven. On one occasion in late 1974, a man who had been acting and responding sexually identified himself as an undercover police officer. He informed me that I was under arrest for lewd conduct in a public accommodation. I was, of course, terrified, envisioning the loss of my family and the destruction of my career. Between the rest room and his patrol car, just as he was about to handcuff me, I talked him out of taking me to the station by forswearing returning to the rest stop, which at that moment seemed both prudent and the last thing I would ever want to do again.

It was customary for the *New Haven Register* to print the names of those who had been charged with criminal offenses, and I had always taken special note of those booked on morals charges. I realized I had placed myself in a situation that had endangered me. I also understood that I must be feeling guilty about my sexuality to have done so and that it had been fear of being discovered that made anonymous encounters the only available way I could have sex. I knew that I would have to find ways to express my sexual desire that would put me in less danger and be more fulfilling. The alternative of not expressing it at all and once again labeling myself as "sick" was no longer possible. My near arrest had shocked me into a pellucid understanding of the practical and psychological dangers inherent in remaining closeted.

Emboldened by the American Psychiatric Association's 1973 decision to remove homosexuality from its *Diagnostic and Statistical Manual,* I began to think about the antihomosexual bias of psychoanalysis and how the view that homosexuals were perverted and should be cured of their illness contributed to the negative image gay men and lesbians have of themselves. I recognized that this bias, which I and my analyst shared, had caused neither of us to question at any time during nearly ten years of treatment why I was suppressing my homosexuality and why I was not permitting myself to have sexual contact with men.

I did not write about these issues for another decade because I was interested in professional advancement, my colleagues' approval, and developing a private practice. Being part of an orthodox Freudian psychoanalytic group, although one more tolerant of divergent views than many other analytic societies, I knew I would be considered too inexperienced to have a valuable opinion about any controversial theoretical or clinical issue. Any such views would simply have been dismissed and would have raised questions about my own sexual orientation.

Over the next few years I wrote and published articles on traditional analytic subjects and became active in the psychoanalytic institute and society. I was appointed to the institute's faculty and Board of Trustees, in 1978 was elected president of the society, and the next year was appointed to important committees of both the American Psychoanalytic and International Psychoanalytical associations.

Feeling isolated by my career and being married and still haunted by the memory of nearly having been arrested, I felt it was essential for my emotional health to share my life as a homosexual with others who could be affirming of my sexual orientation. I had no friends or colleagues with whom I felt comfortable talking about my experiences. I could not speak with my analyst, who would believe I was acting out my anxiety and anger and recommend that I reenter analysis. Nor was I yet prepared to talk with my wife.

In 1978 I cautiously began to cruise in New Haven. On one occasion I met a younger, married member of Yale's psychiatry department who, calling himself "bisexual," informed me that there were several other psychiatrists that he knew personally who were married and either gay or bisexual. They met periodically for lunch to provide support for one another, and I immediately made myself known to each of them.

All of these colleagues were respected professionals; two were also members of the psychoanalytic society. Like myself, they were living double lives and having sexual encounters that at one time or another had placed them in physical danger or legal jeopardy. By then I was clearly aware of the role that my childhood, society's prejudice, and my own analysis had played in causing me to deny my homosexuality. I knew that my view that homosexuality was a sickness had been one manifestation of my self-hatred. I recognized that my readiness to change and my willingness to submit to a treatment aimed at doing so had also been symptoms of my injured self-esteem. I was, therefore, distressed by how fearful each of us was of being discovered, and I was troubled by the deception we were engaged in to sustain our professional and personal lives.

I was particularly distressed by the effect that my secretiveness was having on my clinical work. By attempting to protect myself from patients' curiosity and scrutiny out of fear that my homosexuality would be exposed, I was never responsive to questions about my personal life. I had, of course, rationalized my need for anonymity as serving my patients' need for an ambiguous object on whom they could project their own fantasies. But my rigidity in this regard was often unnecessarily depriving and sometimes hindered their treatment. I recognized that my energy was being diverted in the clinical situation from self-reflection to self-protection and that fear of being discovered was often interfering with my capacity for empathic response and spontaneity when it was clinically appropriate. The need to hide my sexual orientation was gradually eroding my sense of personal integrity and thereby compromising the honesty that is necessary to sustain the therapeutic endeavor and that contributes to its effectiveness. I became determined to be more out as a gay man.

I knew that to be more self-affirming it would be necessary to find gay friends who were open and more comfortable with their sexual orientation than those I had met in New Haven. I had my first opportunity to come out to an openly gay man in 1979, when I met Larry Kramer at a party given by his former therapist and his wife. I had recently read his novel, *Faggots,* found it caustic and honest, and arranged to meet him at his apartment the next day. When I told him I was gay, Larry attacked me for being closeted and in a profession that had "fucked him up." He told me that the reason I was still closeted was that I was afraid I would lose my patients. He also said I should get divorced. I knew he was partly correct: I was concerned about losing patients. But I did not want a divorce and was concerned about the effect coming out would have on my marriage.

Larry's anger spewed out relentlessly. At the time, of course, I did not know that he would make continued creative use of this anger in his writing and, a few years later, in starting two important organizations, Gay Men's Health Crisis (GMHC) and ACT UP. I wondered only whether all future experiences of coming out would make people so angry and be so painful. But I liked his honesty and admired his incisive intelligence. I have felt bonded to him over the years, not only because of my unabashed, if somewhat wary, admiration but because my analyst, Larry told me, had been his therapist when he was a Yale undergraduate.

A few weeks later, while in New York attending professional meetings, I went to a bar where I met a tall, slender man with beautiful auburn hair and striking brown and olive-green eyes. He was bright and inquisitive, and his capacity for self-reflection and understanding was immediately evident. Aside from his perceptiveness and sense of humor, Gordon was affectionate, emotionally expressive, candid, and utterly without artifice. Since he was many years younger than I and we came from very different backgrounds, I thought I had met only an intelligent friend with whom I could also have enjoyable sexual encounters. Over the following year I found our differences interesting and that they enhanced the relationship. I was surprised when I discovered that our mutual attachment had deepened and I had fallen in love.

Not long after meeting Gordon, I read a letter in *The New York Times* from Frank Rundle, who had identified himself as president of the Association of Gay Psychiatrists. I called Frank and made plans to speak with him and the president-elect of the association, David Kessler, at the forthcoming meetings of the American Psychiatric Association in San Francisco in May 1980.[2]

Frank and David were the first openly gay mental health

professionals with whom I had an opportunity to speak. We shared convictions about the mental health benefits of being out and the need for social and political change within and outside of psychiatry. Their nonjudgmental attitude, understanding, and concern about my difficult social and professional situations were in striking contrast to the attitudes of the closeted psychiatrists and analysts I knew in New Haven, who seemed to view my need to be more open as recklessly endangering my career and marriage and also to be concerned about their exposure were I to become more out.

In 1980, my wife joined me at the psychiatry meetings in San Francisco, where I told her that I was homosexual. Although I did not want a divorce, since I was devoted to her and our sons, then ten and fourteen, it was no longer possible for me to hide my sexual orientation. I believed at the time that it would be possible to be out, when honesty and integrity demanded, and to maintain a viable marriage.

I told her everything I believed she should know about my past and current life, including my relationship with Gordon, that might help her decide about the future direction of her own life and, specifically, whether she wanted to remain in our marriage. My wife was initially relieved that she had not been responsible for my sexual unresponsiveness and appeared to understand both that I needed to express my sexuality and that I loved her and our boys. However, over the next months she made it clear that she wanted me to keep my homosexuality secret to maintain the privacy of the family. We cared a lot about each other and hoped to be able to maintain the relationship, but I feared that her need for secrecy and my need to make my sexual orientation a more positive and better integrated aspect of my self would eventually cause conflict and discord.

Over the next few years, Gordon was often angry about my

desire to remain with my family, but he remained respectful of my feelings, agreeing to keep our times together constant each week and careful not to intrude on my life at home. His willingness to sacrifice his own needs for mine meant a great deal, and his thoughtfulness enabled my marriage to continue with reasonable comfort for a few more years.

My family and I moved from New Haven to New York in 1981, after I had spent a year commuting to begin a practice in New York. I started to see many gay men, sent to me by straight colleagues who did not know I was gay. By that time I was responding honestly to inquiries about my sexual orientation, all of which were made by gay patients. My straight patients assumed I was heterosexual because I wore a wedding band, and there were then no known homosexual analysts. My gay patients, generally relieved and pleased that I was also gay, told friends and colleagues. I increasingly got more self-referred patients, particularly those who were mental health workers themselves, and my sexual orientation gradually became known.

Since I was chairperson of the American Psychoanalytic Association's Program Committee and secretary of the International Psychoanalytical Association's Program Committee, I now felt I was in a better professional position to raise questions and share what I was learning about the clinical treatment and development of gay men, which had, of course, been importantly shaped by my own experience. I was also in a better personal position to do so since I was out to my wife. For the December 1983 meeting of the American Psychoanalytic Association, I organized and chaired a panel on male homosexuality where I challenged the view of homosexuality as perversion and spoke about some of the men I had seen whose previous analysts had caused psychological damage by attempting to change their sexual orientation.[3] Before that meeting I had had referrals from heterosexual colleagues; afterward, the referrals almost completely ceased. The change in attitude was caused both by colleagues becoming more attentive to rumors about my homosexuality and by my harsh criticism of traditional psychoanalytic theory and practice.

In 1986 I decided to tell my former analyst that I was gay. We had become friendly after I finished my training and occasionally had family dinners and celebrated significant family events together. In spite of my anger at him for not helping me to accept my homosexuality, I liked him, and had become fond of his family and felt that he had helped me in my analysis in other important ways.

I told Ruben about my relationship with Gordon, my increasing need to be out within the gay community, and being more withdrawn and less available to my wife. He looked distressed but had little to say except that he hoped I would be able to live my life in a way that was satisfactory. Our meeting was more perfunctory than I had wished, and sensing his discomfort, I said that I would like to speak with him further and perhaps he could call me whenever he had the time to do so. The call was not forthcoming. I wrote to him, wanting to heal the rift that I felt had been caused by my revelation, mentioned that my life was complex and difficult but challenging and happy and that I was, for the time being, content. He never responded to my letter. I called to ask that he give me a call so we could get together when he was in New York City, but he never did. At its end this relationship recapitulated the rejection I had experienced with my father.

My wife and I had made the decision not to tell the boys about my homosexuality until they seemed developmentally prepared to deal with it. We worked to continue to provide a secure and loving home for them for as long as we could. But in 1987 our older son, who was then twenty-one, accidentally discovered that Gordon and I had been on a trip together. We then told him I was gay and had an ongoing relationship with Gordon. Our younger son had just left for his first year of college, and we decided not to speak with him until he returned for Christmas vacation. At the time divorce was not imminent, and we reassured them. But both boys were angry and upset, not so much at my being gay as at feeling betrayed by my secret life and by the appearance of a happy marriage. I believe our decision not to burden either them or the marriage by telling them had been correct, but I also believe that the secrecy has had the lasting effect of making them less trusting of their perceptions of their world.

The boys' knowledge undoubtedly made easier my wife's growing conviction that it was untenable for her to stay in a marriage that was making her increasingly unhappy. The next year she asked me for a divorce. I was distressed by losing someone I still cared about and had shared so much with, but I was also relieved and excited by the prospect of the future—having a more authentic life, living with Gordon, and defining new roles, socially and within my profession.

2 The Gay Therapist

*Certainly in order to be able to go out to the other you must have the
starting place, you must have been, you must be, with yourself.*
— MARTIN BUBER

Many of the patients I started to see in New York in
1980 were gay, referred by straight colleagues who wanted to
help me start a practice. For a few months I did not respond to
patients' questions about my own sexual orientation, rationalizing that to do otherwise would distort the transference by not
presenting a blank screen on whom they could project their
own fantasies. In fact, since some of my patients were themselves mental health workers, I was concerned that knowledge
of my homosexuality would get back to my colleagues and
referrals would cease. But I also realized that not responding
honestly to my patients' curiosity about my sexual orientation
was interfering with my capacity to be spontaneous and with

my ability to be empathic because I was diverting so much energy and attention to hiding and disguising myself. After recognizing that my effectiveness as a therapist was being compromised by my anxiety about being discovered, I started to respond directly to my patients' inquiries about whether I was also homosexual. I had not fully appreciated at the time how eager many gay men are to be treated by a gay therapist.

After I presented my paper on male homosexuality at the December 1983 meeting of the American Psychoanalytic Association, more gay men began to seek treatment, eager to talk to a traditionally trained psychoanalyst who viewed their sexuality as a normal variant of human sexuality. Within the next year or two many also sought analysis or therapy because they had heard I was gay.

When gay men seek analysis or therapy from a gay therapist, they do so because of concern that the heterosexual bias of most therapists will interfere with their being treated with appropriate neutrality. For if any therapist adheres to the orthodox psychoanalytic theory that the only normal developmental pathway leads to heterosexuality, even if he attempts to be nonjudgmental it will be difficult for him to act in a neutral manner. He will be unable to ask the necessary questions and make the clarifying interpretations that will help his patients feel less inhibited or in less conflict about their homosexuality. Even if he does not attempt to change his patients' sexual orientation, such a therapist is likely to convey a heterosexual bias inadvertently through comments, suggestion, or tone and thereby to increase his patients' shame or guilt.[1]

Gay men and lesbians also often feel that there are specific developmental and social issues confronting them of which straight analysts and dynamically oriented therapists have little knowledge. There is appropriate concern among knowledgeable homosexual patients that the lack of clinical and personal familiarity with their developmental issues may lead to incorrect or biased assumptions, interpretations, and formulations. For example, the special nature of the early erotic attachment of the male child to his father and the ways in which the repression of this attachment may influence later relationships, the nature and importance of coming out first to oneself and then to others, the effect of social and peer stigmatization on self-esteem, and the particular nature of gay relationships and how they differ from conventional heterosexual relationships are a few important aspects of development about which most analysts are not knowledgeable. Better-informed gay men, particularly those who are themselves in the mental health field, have become increasingly discriminating about the level of knowledge and expertise of the analyst or therapist from whom they seek assistance.

Those gay men who seek therapy from a psychoanalyst or an analytically oriented therapist do so because they believe that an explorative therapy will be most helpful for the neurotic or character problems that are affecting the quality of their relationships or their productivity in work-related endeavors.[2] Most do not view their homosexuality as a problem, and they are not seeking to alter their sexual orientation. However, some analysts will still argue that an attitude on the part of the patient that excludes investigation of the pathological origin of his sexual orientation and the possibility of change precludes a successful treatment and indicates that the patient is not analyzable.[3] I have presented a very different view based upon my clinical experience. If a gay man wishes to change his sexual orientation, it is usually because early self-esteem injury and the internalization of social bias have resulted in an inability to consolidate and integrate his sexual orientation during adolescence and early adulthood, causing the instability of his homosexual identity.

The Analyst's Disclosure of His Homosexuality

Most patients entering therapy assume that their analyst or therapist is heterosexual. Patients make this assumption in part because they believe that gay men and lesbians would not be in this position of authority and prestige. There is also a commonly held belief that homosexuals are more emotionally disturbed than heterosexuals. Since patients are predisposed to idealize the emotional health of their caregivers they are further inclined to believe their therapist is heterosexual. There are still relatively few gay and lesbian therapists who identify themselves as such. Their lack of visibility reinforces the assumption of therapists' heterosexuality.

The heterosexual assumption is most commonly made by heterosexual patients, but it is also made by many gay men and lesbians who, internalizing society's prejudice, believe that they are defective or sick. They feel that if the therapist is not heterosexual, he must also be defective.

The gay analyst's or therapist's disclosure of his sexual orientation at an appropriate point in therapy is necessary and important for effective therapy with any gay patient. It provides him with the positive role model that many gay men lack. Analyzing their feelings about working with a gay therapist helps most patients undo the negative stereotypes and internalized homophobia inevitably acquired living in a prejudiced society.

Alan, who had been in an analytically oriented therapy intermittently for many years with a highly regarded psychoanalyst, left that treatment because he felt his therapist had depreciated his attempts to express his homosexuality. He had had almost exclusively homoerotic fantasies for as long as he could remember and had had periodic gay experiences in high school. However, he had dated several women because he wanted to please and be accepted by his peers and was afraid of alienating his emotionally distant mother and very demanding, critical father. Because he longed for his father's love and acceptance and feared complete rejection if he became openly gay, Alan continued to date, then married, and had one child. While he was married, he continued to have sex at bathhouses and pick up men at gay bars. It was the anxiety and unhappiness caused by this double life that led him to divorce and, several years later, to seek treatment from his first therapist.

In the prior therapy, he had gained considerable understanding of his masochistic attachment to both of his parents; he learned of many ways he had of sabotaging his own happiness and success. However, Alan also continued to conceal most of his homosexual desire and experiences from his therapist because he believed that the analyst was subtly, and at times overtly, critical of them. He felt totally alone with the passion he felt for men and began to believe that his analyst had little understanding of or empathy with his homosexual life. He felt he should see a therapist who was more accepting, more empathic, and more knowledgeable about his sexual orientation.

When he first came to see me, although believing I was homosexual, he made no direct inquiry about my sexual orientation. When he did, several months after beginning treatment, it was due to his anger at my not volunteering this information and to his growing awareness that he was reluctant to inquire. After we learned what had been inhibiting his inquiry, and believing that not responding directly would serve no further useful purpose, I did tell him that I was gay. Initially he expressed considerable relief, stating that at last he could express himself and be understood. He felt that he had never had gay role models and that being homosexual had simply meant having sex with another man. He was excited by the prospect of experiencing an emotional connection with another man who, like himself, was gay.

In subsequent hours Alan became quite anxious. My confirming that I was also homosexual had evoked in him a longing to be close to me. Then he wondered whether he was making a mistake seeing me and began to express some anger and contempt. Over time he was grateful for my directness and relieved at being in treatment, but was frightened by his many strong feelings.

Particular to the childhood of homosexual boys is that their fathers often become detached, hostile, or rejecting toward them during their early years. They perceive that their son is different from other boys, often having less traditionally male interests. Some of these fathers may withdraw because consciously or unconsciously they recognize the boy's erotic attachment or desire for closeness. Alan's father started to withdraw when Alan was about five, favoring an older female sibling, because he thought Alan effeminate. Alan began to realize that any intimacy with another man evoked both a longing and the conviction that he would eventually be rejected, as he felt he had been by his father. It was this conviction that caused the contempt that had disrupted all past relationships and was beginning to threaten the stability of his relationship with his current lover, as well as with me.

It is possible that a heterosexual therapist who was appropriately free of bias could also have provided the environment in which Alan would have been able to experience and express projections of his own self-hatred and internalized homophobia in the transference. But this man needed a therapist who could also provide the necessary empathy and sensitivity to the issues of his past and current life to help him make the transition to a life with a lover, including knowledge of and a non-judgmental attitude toward the varieties of forms of intimacy in gay relationships.

Most important, working with a gay man gave Alan the opportunity to have the positive role model he felt he had always lacked, for the absence of identifiable models in the life of most gay men, particularly during their adolescence and young adulthood, makes the positive image of the gay analyst or therapist a valuable part of any therapy for most homosexual patients. It is of particular value for mental health workers: the consolidation and positive integration of their gay identity is important not only for their emotional maturation and well-being but for their effective functioning as therapists.

Identification with the therapist's empathy, thoughtfulness, and psychological curiosity is important for any patient, heterosexual or homosexual, if he is to do the difficult work of observing and understanding his own feelings during the treatment itself and to continue to do so after termination. Essential to establishing and maintaining this identification are the perception and conviction of the therapist's integrity, not only around issues of his persevering psychological curiosity but also concerning those aspects of his character and life that are unfailingly revealed in the intimacy of the therapeutic relationship. When a gay therapist chooses not to acknowledge to his patients that he is homosexual because of shame or fear of exposure, he is failing to provide the model of personal integrity that is essential for the difficult self-scrutiny of any successful therapy. As Freud wrote, "We must not forget that the analytic relationship is based on a love of truth . . . and that it precludes any kind of sham or deceit."[4]

I am not suggesting that the usual uncovering and interpretive work of any dynamic therapy is not of major importance in working with gay men. I am not advocating a precipitous acquiescence to any patient's request for information without eliciting fantasies and associations over an appropriate period of time. I am convinced, however, that the gay analyst or therapist who hides or disguises his sexual orientation does further damage to his patients' self-esteem by conveying his own shame, self-depreciation, or fear of disclosure. Equally important, he fails to provide a corrective for his patients' injured self-esteem that in part derives from internalized social attitudes and parental and peer rejection.

Benjamin, for example, was an experienced therapist who sought consultation with me primarily because of problems in his relationship of many years, as well as conflict around his homosexuality in general. He had told me of difficulties he was having working with some of the clinical problems of his patients because of concern that he might reveal his familiarity with certain aspects of their gay life and that his patients would then infer that he was homosexual. On one occasion he felt obliged to hide from a patient that he understood an idiosyncratic sexual term and on several occasions concealed his familiarity with the gay bars his patient mentioned. He believed that self-revelation or the discovery by the patient of his homosexuality would interfere with being a blank screen and with the transference. His anxiety, however, had caused him to become more and more reluctant to accept gay referrals and to be increasingly uncomfortable working with the gay patients he already had.

This man felt that he had been in a successful treatment, completed three years before he saw me. He had heard rumors of his first analyst's homosexuality and had even been told by a colleague that he had seen his analyst in a gay bar while at a meeting in another city. On several occasions, Benjamin had confronted him with these rumors; in response, however, the analyst had either remained silent or asked him questions about his fantasies.

In our work together over a period of about one year, Benjamin was able to talk about how he had felt deceived by his analyst, while also acknowledging how in other ways he had been knowledgeable and helpful. His analyst's discomfort with his own homosexuality had reinforced Benjamin's self-depreciatory views and attitudes, contributing to the difficulty he was experiencing working with his gay patients. When he did treat gay men, he found himself adopting his therapist's refusal to answer questions about his own sexual orientation. The result was that some patients left him, and his work was anxiety-ridden and not as gratifying as it might otherwise have been.

One might wonder whether the revelation of sexual orientation is not a rationalized, self-indulgent manifestation of a countertransference need to please or be seductive. Reflection on my own work and the work of supervisees has indicated that the therapist's self-revelation is not overly gratifying to the patient; it does not lead most patients to have unrealistic expectations of the capacity or willingness of the analyst to satisfy needs and longings, nor is it usually perceived as being seductive.

A homosexual patient may have a need to please his heterosexual therapist by attempting to become straight.[5] In my experience treating heterosexual patients and hearing about them from other gay therapists, I have never heard of a heterosexual patient attempting to become gay. There is too much social disapproval to do so, and gay therapists are, in my experience, very careful not to engage in such suasion, contrary to society's expectation and that of some heterosexual therapists as well.

The following case illustrates that even a homosexual

patient's knowledge of my sexual orientation did not prompt him to want to become gay, but it was nevertheless of thera-peutic value.

A forty-six-year-old married man with one child had been in analytically oriented therapy for several years before consulting me after the sudden death of his therapist. Neither Peter nor the referring analyst knew at that time that I was homosexual.*

He had last had sex with another man two years after finish-ing college and shortly before marrying. He felt extremely guilty about his former homosexual activity as well as about his current exclusively homoerotic fantasies and his attraction to other men. He believed his homosexuality made him bad.

His relationship with his wife was poor. They had not had sex for fifteen years, following the birth of their only child. Pro-jecting a good deal of his anger and guilt onto her, he spent a lot of time at job-related activities, attempting to avoid her crit-icism. Throughout the first four years of our work Peter saw me as an idealized parent. I could make no mistakes, no incorrect or inadequate interpretations, no errors of judgment; he was oblivious of me as a person with human attributes, it seemed clear that he dared not risk seeing me in a real way for fear that any perception of a defect would so infuriate him that it would destroy our relationship. Interpretation of this aspect of the transference was met only with his denial and rationalization.

Over the years he had wondered whether I was gay. He would mention this when he saw other obviously gay patients in my waiting room. Once he saw me with my lover outside the office and said hello, but the next day recollected that I had been alone.

During the fifth year of therapy, after the publication of my

---

*For the past twenty years every gay patient who has sought my help has known my sexual orientation.

book *Being Homosexual* in 1989, he hesitantly but directly asked me whether I was gay, and I then responded equally directly to his question. He told me over several hours that he was scornful, particularly because I could not be "macho." He hated homosexuality because it was a sign of femininity in men. Some sessions later, for the first time, he mentioned that he believed his father, who preferred an older sibling, hated him for not being more masculine. He wanted, he said, for me to love and accept him as his father had been unable to do.

Over the next many months he became more accepting of his homosexuality, grew much less critical of himself, and stopped believing he was bad for having homosexual fantasies. He began to deal in an effective and, at times, moving way with the perceived rejection by both his parents. The relationship with his wife, although remaining asexual, did improve. He chose, however, not to have homosexual sex. He did not want to disrupt the relationship with his wife, a source of stability and comfort, but even more important, he feared the possible scorn and rejection of colleagues.

Chapter 4 deals with the special problems of heterosexually married homosexual men, including Peter's. Here I am emphasizing that my revealing I was homosexual was beneficial because it enabled Peter to articulate his feared anger without its disrupting his relationship with me. And although knowing I was gay helped him become more accepting of his homosexual fantasies and feelings, it did not cause him to attempt to have gay sex.

It may also be important for therapy with heterosexual patients for the therapist to reveal his sexual orientation if he happens to be gay.

For several months, one man had been curious about my office, books, furniture, and especially about a second room, where he occasionally used the telephone to call his own office.

He was like a detective looking for clues. When I made this observation, he acknowledged that he was inquisitive about me, but he was uncertain what he was so curious about.

After the publication of *Being Homosexual,* he asked me whether I was gay, saying that my well-known interest in gay men must have some important roots in my own life. I asked him what he thought, but he was unable to say much, and during the following several weeks our work came to a virtual standstill. Finally, I wondered if his concern about my being homosexual made it difficult for him to talk. He said that it did and wanted to know why I was avoiding answering his question. He commented that it made him feel I was hiding something that I was ashamed of revealing. I interpreted that he might be ashamed of and afraid of revealing aspects of his own sexuality, which was correct but not helpful. I was rationalizing my concern about this heterosexual man's response to my being gay, including the possibility that he would leave treatment, by making it appear that he was simply projecting his shame onto me.

After several more weeks of unproductive sessions, I did answer his question. There were a few perfunctory questions about my life and then a sigh of considerable relief. His subsequent hours took a dramatic turn. He spoke for the first time of sadomasochistic heterosexual fantasies that he had found troublesome throughout his life. He saw them as perverse. In general he became more comfortable and less constricted in expressing his feelings and thoughts. When I inquired several months later about the change in the quality of our work, he commented that he had always felt I was too conventional to be able to understand his sadomasochistic fantasies. This belief, of course, had important transference implications; to some extent it derived from his projected self-criticism and shame. But my failure to be responsive to his questions had led to a stalemated treatment because it reinforced his sense of shame and lack of trust in my veracity. Acknowledgment of my homosexuality, which he had long suspected, enabled him to understand and accept his own forbidden fantasies and then to feel less inhibited and take more pleasure in sex with his wife.

Another heterosexual patient, who had been in analysis for six years, saw me as being uninterested, distant, cold, and uncaring, like his self-involved father. He also knew of my work and had heard I was homosexual but did not want to know with certainty. He said, "If you were gay, I'd like you better. I told Roger [a gay friend] that I didn't know for certain. If you were, I wouldn't invest you with so much; I couldn't feel you were so cold and uninterested. I couldn't feel you were always telling me what I should do, how I should behave. I wouldn't have to be such a schmuck here."

Over time he became less frightened of and angry about his affectionate, loving, erotic wishes and longings for his father and, in the transference, for me. Then he was able to ask me if I was gay. My being gay, he said, meant being capable, unlike his father, of tolerating his desire for closeness. Not responding to his question at this point would only have reinforced his defensive need to experience me as depriving.

Not all heterosexual patients, however, have used the knowledge or suspicion of my homosexuality to benefit their therapy. Donald, familiar with my patient population and with my writing, wondered for some time whether I was gay. He had a very correct, moralistic attitude about his own life and consequently about others. Not too long after the publication of my book he announced that he wanted to stop therapy. There had been no suggestion of this heretofore, and our work, spanning many years, had been successful in most respects. He wanted to stop, he said, because he felt that I was critical of him, especially his need for upward mobility and for social and professional acceptance.

He had spoken during the course of his long therapy of his disgust at homosexual behavior and of his phobic concerns that he or a member of his family could get AIDS from associating with gay men. Several times he wondered whether I was gay but stated that he did not want to know. He was afraid that he would perceive me as diminished, insignificant, and disgusting if he found out that I was.

Displacement of rage stemming from a frustrated desire for closeness to his emotionally distant, frequently absent father manifested itself as criticism of men he perceived as being in positions of authority. He was contemptuous of his desire for affection from and closeness to them and me, and this contempt was sometimes expressed in the transference as homophobia. In many ways his therapy was successful, and he did gain some understanding of the extent of his anger at and longing for his father. However, because of the intensity of his anxiety over the conflicted, positive erotized transference, these feelings were incompletely worked through and contributed to his termination of treatment.

I can also confirm from my clinical experience that feelings about the homosexuality of the therapist may be a source of resistance and anxiety for some gay men as well. My understanding of and interest in the developmental issues of gay men and my expressed concern for their therapeutic well-being have been important reasons for many to seek treatment with me. However, years of feeling alienated or rejected, causing some to be secretive about their sexuality, may prompt them to feel anxiety and conflict about the possibility of seeing another gay man. This manifestation of transference, when it occurs, is most frequently caused either by their projected self-contempt or by the abrupt awakening of repressed longings for the father. If anxiety is evoked by working with a gay therapist, it must be interpreted early, for when the anxiety is severe and occurs before the development of a therapeutic alliance, it may lead to an abrupt termination. I have done several consultations with gay men where I believe the anxiety caused by my also being gay was a factor in their decision not to return for treatment.

For some gay men who were in analysis or therapy with me, anxiety about my being homosexual led to resistance and stalemated treatment. One man knew that the psychiatrist who referred him to me believed he should be treated by a gay therapist. He was also aware of the predominantly gay nature of my practice and had been told by another patient that I was gay. Nevertheless, he steadfastly maintained that I was heterosexual. When confronted with his denial, he expressed concern that if he were certain I was gay, his derision and contempt would cause him to leave therapy. After he asked me and I told him I was gay, we were able to understand that his anxiety about my homosexuality was determined by a number of factors, including the contempt he felt for his demeaned father, the need to distance himself from affectionate and erotic longings for his father, and projections of his own internalized homophobia. But the intensity of the transference did not lead to the disruption of treatment, and his feelings about me and my homosexuality were a significant and productive part of the work of his therapy.

The following case further illustrates how a gay patient's anxiety about my sexual orientation caused resistance and that understanding the reasons for this resistance was of great importance to the treatment.

Edward, a psychiatrist, was thirty-two when he entered treatment. He had felt hurt and angry when a colleague had spoken in a deprecatory manner of homosexuals. Although he lived openly with his lover, he generally kept his homosexuality secret at work. He experienced his sexual orientation as normal for him; but he nevertheless held to a pathological model of homosexuality and he believed his teachers and supervisors, who had taught him that homosexuality was a perversion and a symptom that resulted from a developmental fixation.*

He had wondered whether I was gay from being familiar with my papers and from what he had heard from others, but, because I was a psychoanalyst and married at the time, he thought I must be straight. Like the previous patient, he needed to believe I was heterosexual in order to contain hostility that he feared could destroy his relationship with me. Edward was convinced that I would not be able to tolerate his rage and contempt and that I would "fire him" from therapy if he expressed these emotions.

Treatment was stalemated for several months because of his need to deny my homosexuality. Interpretation, intended to point out the fear of his own rage, was also greeted with denial. At some point, when he asked me directly, I did confirm that I was homosexual. He was startled and furious, derisive and contemptuous.

The work that followed, though, suggested that the confrontation had provided a needed breakthrough in his treatment. He began to talk with more affect about his early relationship with his depressed mother, whose withdrawal, self-involvement, and lack of interest had made him feel he was bad and defective. It became clear that feelings of being defective had been displaced onto his sexuality, and to some extent they accounted for his hatred of his own homosexuality and his

---

*It is much less common now than it was in the 1980s for psychiatry residents to be taught that homosexuality is a symptom of emotional illness.

homophobia. He began to be more comfortable about bringing his hostility and aggression into the hour after he understood their relationship to his mother's neglect and the frustration of early needs. Difficulty in expressing his own anger did not cease, however, since his fear that he would harm me was also related to his continued attachment to his erratically impulsive, occasionally abusive father, an issue not understood until much later in treatment.

Transference Elaboration

It has generally been believed a priori that disclosure of one's sexual orientation, or, for that matter, any details of one's life, interferes with the development and elaboration of the transference because the therapist ceases to be a blank screen on whom the patient can project, unencumbered, his own fears, wishes, and conflicts. In my experience working with gay men, transference wishes and feelings continue to be elaborated throughout the therapy unabated and unaffected by knowledge of my sexual orientation.

A patient who knew I was gay had heard from a colleague that I had gone to a professional meeting with my lover. After hearing this, he became preoccupied with how busy I was professionally, how complicated my life was, and how little energy I must have for my patients. He had a difficult time talking, and he was noticeably tense and emotionally withdrawn during the hour. In sessions during the subsequent weeks he had more difficulty articulating feelings; he was very detached. After several weeks he began to recall something he had mentioned in his early hours but had not brought up again: during his childhood his mother and father had left him each weekend with his grandmother. He had felt abandoned, jealous, and deprived. At this stage in his treatment his transference was maternal. He experienced me as cold and depriving, like his depressed, preoccupied, withdrawn mother. He felt that like her I was secretive and ungiving. At other times in his analysis he perceived me as like his abusive, uncaring father, who was often absent and emotionally unavailable, in part because of his frequent affairs. Because of pressure to express these old feelings, the same distortions would have occurred if I had been heterosexual.

Another patient, who had been told I was homosexual by a colleague early in his therapy, also illustrates how tenacious the transference is and how difficult it is to disrupt or distort it. After he had speculated for some time about my sexual orientation, I responded to his direct question, confirming what he had already been told, believing that failure to do so would be harmful to him in the ways discussed before.

During much of his therapy he had been preoccupied with his longing for his father, who favored a more troubled, more masculine older sibling. In his third year of analysis, in the throes of being very angry with me because he was convinced I favored other patients, he came to one hour with his fly unzipped. Early in the hour, seemingly unaware of his unzipped fly, he spoke of his father's loving women. He knew that his father had had a few affairs during his childhood; he would like to be a woman, he said, "like one of those women who took my father away from me." When I called his attention to his open fly, he said it felt like a dress unzipped up the side.

"I'd like to be a girl and have all these hot guys attracted to me." He was enacting with me his desire for his father and his childhood wishes of wanting to be like the women who'd had his father's attention. The transference persevered in spite of his knowing that, unlike his father, I would be more interested in him as a man than as a woman.

Yet another patient, a man of about twenty-eight, knew I was gay and spoke about it with seeming comfort, pleased to be working with me. In his second year of treatment he became certain I was critical and dismissive of him for being homosexual. He said that he had difficulty seeing me as a gay man and at times wondered whether, in fact, I was gay. His powerful denial arose because of the persistent need to see me as being like his angry, critical, dismissive father, a perception unshaken by his knowledge that I was also gay. Of course, this aspect of the transference was of great value in helping him to understand how his old relationship with his father had interfered with his capacity to form intimate relationships as an adult.

Knowledge of the therapist's sexual orientation, like any other information that a patient acquires about his analyst or therapist, will not disrupt the treatment process if the therapist uses such information in the service of the collaborative work, and if the well-being of the patient and the therapy remain in the forefront of the therapist's mind. The cooperation of the patient in making use of such information depends upon his feeling that he is in a comfortable, safe, and trusting relationship with someone of personal integrity. When the primary motive of the analyst or therapist in revealing a significant part of his life is his own and not his patient's well-being, or when a fact is inadvertently discovered and the therapist either responds defensively or shuns acknowledging the truth of the patient's perception or knowledge, then I believe the transference will be significantly impaired. The therapist will usually be perceived as the parent who made the patient feel helpless by distorting reality or by making the child feel he could not trust his own perceptions. Similarly, when information is offered excessively or gratuitously in order to appease the patient, ward off anger, or be seductive, the therapist will be seen as manipulative and dishonest, and anxiety and anger may thwart the progress of treatment, including the development of the transference.

Countertransference

To be a gay man in the profession of psychoanalysis and, to a lesser extent, in psychiatry, psychology, or social work, may be isolating. There is always the countertransference temptation to use one's gay patients or clients to counter this sense of professional isolation. Revealing one's sexual orientation may at times be in the service of establishing a sense of social alliance with one's patients. Every gay therapist should be aware that such needs may influence his decision to reveal his sexual orientation. Obviously, such gratification should not be the primary motive for self-revelation. On the other hand, the anticipation of obtaining gratification should not inhibit the therapist from self-revelation that is in the patient's interest.

Countertransference issues may also arise when patients respond to the discovery of the therapist's homosexuality with homophobic attitudes. At times, as I illustrated before, one has to deal with the internalized homophobia of gay patients, which may be expressed in demeaning or denigrating comments. Such attitudes may evoke intense feelings in the therapist.

I told Frank that I was homosexual after he had made several inquiries and after what I believed to have been a thorough investigation of his fantasies over an appropriate period of time. He subsequently became anxious, resentful, and contemptuous and took every opportunity to attempt to humiliate me. The intensity of his feelings was related to his conviction that only a gay man, who was defective as he felt he was, would be interested in spending time with him. He had a special interest in pointing out to me repeatedly that an eminent heterosexual analyst, whom he had seen in consultation before he saw me, had been too busy to work with him. This meant to him that the other analyst must be better than I, an idea he needed to assert repeatedly in order to deny both his sense of feeling rejected by that analyst and his growing sense of attachment to me.

I grew increasingly irritated, not only with his continuing denigration but also because he could not deal with his positive feelings for me. My attempts to help him work with the intensity of the transference by interpreting the humiliation he felt from his father's rejection in childhood were not particularly helpful.

I was little aware of how irritated I was until I began to confuse this man with George, who had sought treatment with me specifically because I was gay. I asked George why he was avoiding any mention of the previous hour when he had been so angry and distressed because of my sexual orientation. Although George had occasionally acknowledged some ambivalent feelings about my sexuality, he said that he believed I was confusing him with someone else. It was only then that I understood I had been avoiding my growing anger at Frank by confusing him with this man, who had been much more accepting of both me and my sexual orientation, and was able to acknowledge to myself my irritation.

The countertransference response that was most disruptive of treatment occurred with the heterosexual patient mentioned earlier in this chapter who feared that physical proximity to gay men might cause some member of his family to get AIDS. He had commented that he would prefer not to live in the same apartment building as gay men because their "promiscuous life style" would hurt the family atmosphere and lower the value of his property. Although we understood that his anxiety about proximity to gays was related, by and large, to his own fears about his femininity and to repressed longings for his father, his homophobia remained an apparently unanalyzable symptom. For a long time I was so angered by his homophobia that I was unable to ask him directly what his articulated hatred of gay men had to do with his thoughts about me. It should have been apparent that I might have moved our work along by a statement that made my sexual orientation specific, clarifying his sadistic need to taunt me because I was homosexual. But my largely unconscious anger toward this man with whom I had worked so hard for many years was so great that I was unable to do this. He terminated treatment prematurely, I believe, in part because of my countertransference difficulty.

Countertransference with AIDS and HIV-Positive Patients

No discussion of countertransference issues of a gay therapist working with gay men is complete without mentioning work with patients who are HIV positive or have AIDS in any of its manifestations. I write in Chapter 5 about the developmental gains these men frequently make after knowing they are infected, particularly their enhanced capacity to fall in love and sustain relationships. Here I want to call attention to how vulnerable to countertransference gay therapists were when AIDS was usually a fatal disease.

Most of the gay patients with the spectrum of HIV-related diseases who were being seen for emotional distress were treated by gay mental health workers. This is appropriate because the empathy, understanding, and sacrifices required of the therapist demand that he have intimate knowledge of the pain, suffering, and emotional and physical devastation caused by the disease.

David had been in analysis for several years in the early 1980s before becoming symptomatic. He had severe narcissistic character pathology with masochistic symptoms that led him to place himself in self-destructive and at times dangerous situations in many aspects of his life, including the seeking of sexual partners. Early in the epidemic, I pointed out to him that the sexual partners he sought out, usually hustlers, many of them intravenous drug users, might be a threat not only to his physical safety but to his health as well. Although he was also a physician, he denied any knowledge of the disease and would not stop behaving self-destructively. While his behavior did begin to modify in the following year, it was not until he noticed swollen lymph nodes and began to have occasional night sweats that he stopped having unsafe sex. When he finally saw a physician and received a diagnosis of cyto-megalovirus of the colon, he developed a calm characteristic of those who have achieved a long-anticipated goal. For him, his disease was punishment for his rage, and his death represented the long-sought destruction of his mother, whom he had identified with and held responsible for his unhappiness.

During his second or third visit to his physician, a specialist in infectious diseases who was involved in AIDS research and treatment, David was advised to go on a trial of a drug that could possibly enhance his flagging immune system. He refused. The exploration of his refusal revealed even more about his ambivalence toward the possibility of getting better. His illness protected him from fear of his mother's rage—he had inflicted on himself what he feared she would eventually do to him. The offer of his physician to place him on a new protocol evoked a recurrent nightmare of a lurking woman with a knife who was going to kill him in his bathtub. He also had a fantasy, which I had not heard since early in his treatment, of being pushed underwater by a mysterious person, probably a woman.

In one hour I expressed my frustration because of his unwillingness to accept help. I was aware that my angry response was partly a displacement of my feeling helpless in the face of this epidemic that was affecting many people I knew. Fears of my own mortality, enhanced by an identification with David, also contributed to the intensity of my feelings.

Several months later, a few weeks before I was to go on my summer holiday, David became sick with a cough, sweats, severe diarrhea, loss of appetite, and a precipitous weight loss. Against his wishes, he was hospitalized and a diagnostic workup revealed that he had several opportunistic infections. It was unclear whether or not he would survive, and during this period, when he was unable to speak with me, I kept in touch with his nurses. About three weeks after entering the hospital, he asked if I would come to see him.

Because I had planned to spend the early part of my holiday in the city, I was able to see him daily in the hospital. He was thin and very pale and had intravenous infusions in both arms. I attempted to hold his hand and to make him more comfortable in his bed. He rebuked me lightly, called the nurse, and asked her to move his bed from the wall to the middle of the floor and to position a chair behind his bed. He asked me to sit behind the bed and to continue his analysis. As best he could, David attempted to free-associate, although his associations were punctuated by requests that I do one thing or another to make him more comfortable, which I was eager to do.

The idea of continuing an analysis with this dying man made me uncomfortable. I felt it was inappropriate. Although he continued to need psychological assistance, I believed that he would now benefit most from a treatment modified from traditional psychoanalysis in order to provide him with necessary support. During this first hour of therapy in the hospital, I asked him why he wanted me behind the bed and to maintain the analytic formality. His response was, "Don't you understand that if you change your role with me now, I'll know you think I'm going to die? I don't want to think about that yet!" The intense distress at seeing my first AIDS patient dying and my anxiety about the possibility that I might have or could acquire the virus had made it impossible to empathize with his need to maintain his denial at that particular time in his illness.

After his release from the hospital, David continued for several weeks to come to my office. He was able to permit me to be more supportive and active and physically helpful. I was able to help him talk about fears of dying and to make practical plans and decisions. In this phase of our work, exploratory therapeutic work did not cease, but his increasing difficulty walking and his decreasing sight demanded supportive and physical interventions on my part when he was in my office. Soon, because of his total loss of vision, he would have to move to the suburbs to be cared for by his parents in their home. In anticipation we cut down the frequency of sessions and set a termination date.

Over the subsequent year I maintained contact with him by telephone. At times he called me; often I called him. We had no established appointments. I intentionally attempted to evolve the analytic relationship into a supportive, warm, and comforting friendship during the last year of his illness, when he was totally blind. He died in early 1989.

Most of us who dealt with AIDS on a daily basis in our practice and in our lives noticed that it affected the way we saw the problems and difficulties of other patients, the uninfected, gay or straight. This work had the effect of decreasing empathy for many of the painful day-to-day problems affecting those patients who were not dying or in acute physical pain. There was the inclination to conserve one's emotional strength in order to be able to give to the most needy by not investing as much in those less in need.

Although HIV/AIDS is now usually a chronic illness because of early detection and effective treatments, many gay therapists, particularly if they see young gay men, are working with patients who again are becoming infected. An awareness of a tendency to be less invested in one's patients generally and of the inclination to defend oneself against the pain of those who are ill has to be maintained if any therapist, and particularly one who is gay, is to continue to work effectively and with maximum sensitivity and empathy. If he does remain emotionally responsive to the anxiety of being confronted with the distress of these patients and those who love them, then it is possible to increase the capacity for empathy and for tolerance of the emotional pain of all human beings.

But dealing with HIV/AIDS has affected the way we see our own lives. The great gift these patients give to those of us who work with them is that they prompt us to look at our lives daily, understanding anew the role that internalized hatred has played, valuing our self-regard and the happiness we have been able to achieve as gay men in a society that can, at times, be so cruel.

3   The Homosexual Adolescent

In the name of what God or what ideal do you forbid me to live according to my nature? And where would my nature lead me if I simply followed it?

—ANDRÉ GIDE

Of the several developmental tasks of adolescence, perhaps the most important is the consolidation of a stable and irreversible sexual identity. In the traditional analytic and developmental literature on adolescence, irreversible sexual identity refers only to the consolidation of heterosexuality.[1] Homosexuality has been considered a developmental failure—specifically, the failure to develop a masculine identity.[2]

The homosexual adolescent enters this period of his life with both burdens and freedoms that most heterosexuals do not share. Many have felt different since childhood, having enjoyed the company of girls more than other boys, being more musical or artistic, more emotionally expressive, and less interested in competitive sports than their peers and male siblings. These perceived distinctions are real; for many homosexual children, they are expressions of their atypical maleness.[3] Many gay adolescents and adults who have repressed their childhood homosexual feelings do recall their atypical behaviors and unconsciously use them to screen out the memory of unwanted early homosexual desire.

Fathers of homosexual children, who may not like their sons being less conventionally masculine than other boys or who are made uncomfortable by their sons' erotic attachment to them or other males, may withdraw from these boys. A homosexual child may also withdraw from his father because he is more comfortable with his mother, has more in common with her, and/or because he is uncomfortable with erotic feelings for his father or the other men around him. The real or perceived rejection by the father because of his child's same-sex desire, different interests, or unconventional maleness is an important factor in the low self-regard of some homosexual boys entering adolescence.[4]

Because they feel different and because of the father's rejection, some homosexual adolescents are more withdrawn or more uncomfortable in peer interactions than their heterosexual counterparts. Feeling like outsiders, they often remain peripheral to the peer groups that are so essential at this stage in helping them separate from parents and feel acceptable and accepted. Therefore, many are forced to become relatively free of reliance on peer approval and more reliant on their own internal resources and judgment than heterosexual boys of the same age.

Social bias, reflected in the attitudes of their parents and peers toward homosexuals, causes many adolescents of twelve, thirteen, fourteen, or fifteen years to repress or suppress their sexual impulses and fantasies and deny to themselves that they are homosexual. Furthermore, homosexual adolescents have few role models; some have a difficult time identifying with those gay men who are visible but who are not conventionally masculine or are socially defiant. And many also equate being homosexual with acquiring AIDS. There are still too few gay athletes, politicians, actors, or celebrated teachers, lawyers, and doctors who come out publicly, believing they have too much to lose. Unfortunately, a homosexual boy in his early adolescence is thereby deprived of those models who might help him acknowledge his homosexuality and enable him to say to himself, "I'm gay like you and want to be like you when I'm older!" As a result of all these factors, most homosexual adolescents hope that their desire for those of the same sex is simply a transient difficulty in a generally troubled period in their lives, a way station to becoming heterosexual.

Many will, therefore, attempt to date and have occasional sex with girls in order to conform to peer, family, and social expectations. Such activities are usually mechanical and passionless efforts that are physically unsuccessful and psychologically distressing. Unsatisfying or failed attempts at heterosexuality make most of these adolescents wonder whether they will ever be capable of a passionate response to another. Feeling sexually unresponsive, many isolate themselves even further from their peers.*

The adolescent most likely to be seen by a traditional therapist or analyst has parents who find their child too effeminate and his suspected sexual orientation unacceptable. They believe he has emotional problems. Their anger or shame contributes to his feeling unappreciated or unloved. He is likely to

---

* Today GLSEN, the Gay, Lesbian and Straight Education Network, is active in many high schools throughout the country, providing education and support for gay students and their straight friends.

have poor self-regard and to denigrate, rather than prize, any unconventional differences he may perceive in himself, especially his sexual orientation.

The homosexual adolescent's uncertainty with regard to his sexual orientation should not, therefore, be understood as conflicted or latent heterosexuality and as an opportunity to dismantle impediments to heterosexuality. Rather, it should be understood as homosexuality inhibited by internal conflict and social bias. Some dynamically oriented therapists inadvertently contribute to delays in acknowledging sexual orientation by encouraging further repression or conscious suppression of homosexual impulses.

In what has been considered a classic paper on the analysis of an adolescent with "homosexual conflicts," Selma Fraiberg reports in admirable detail on her work with her patient Eric,[5] who first entered treatment in prepubescence at age eleven. There had been extensive sex play during childhood between Eric and his brother, Bob, who was two years older than he. This included grabbing and fondling of genitals. While away at camp when he was thirteen, he engaged in horseplay with a counselor, Joe, who snapped the elastic on his swim trunks and fondled his penis. With some reluctance Eric told Dr. Fraiberg that he had invited the sex play and found it exciting. Eric was devoted and attracted to his football coach, whom he longed for and with whom there probably also was sexual activity.

Dr. Fraiberg describes Eric as an "excellent patient from the beginning" since he "found his symptoms very distressing, and was deeply troubled about his cowardice and the implications of sissiness in his behavior."[6] His homosexuality was interpreted as a "passive solution to oedipal rivalry in which he protects himself from castration by surrendering competitive aims." She viewed it as a dangerous, regressive step.

The analysis stopped when he seemed to be more comfortable making overtures to girls. At age seventeen, after he had an ungratifying sexual experience with a prostitute and found "sex wasn't all it was cracked up to be," he returned for some more visits. Eric said that he was now afraid to get close to anyone and was avoiding contact with either sex. Arrangements were made for Eric to go back into analysis with a male colleague of Dr. Fraiberg's when he entered college the next fall.

Dr. Fraiberg believed that her work was successful because it kept Eric from "finding a homosexual partner to whom he was bound through love," thus saving him from acquiring a homosexual identity. Any adolescent with homosexual impulses, she wrote, should be kept from feeling that his homosexual experiences were exciting and satisfying, so that he does not "commit himself through love." She implied that his acknowledged unhappiness from his total lack of attachment was a better outcome than a homosexual one, for his homosexuality was the enemy that "threatens to become victorious" and interferes with the "establishment of the appropriate sexual identification."[7]

We cannot know with certainty, of course, whether or not Eric was homosexual. We do, however, have some suggestion that he was. Dr. Fraiberg tells us that he had a persistent homosexual fantasy life, which he referred to as his homosexual feelings. We are also told that he had an erotic attachment to his father that was both stated and revealed in his dreams. Aspects of this erotic attachment, which is natural in the early life of a homosexual male, were repeated in his erotized relationship with both his counselor and teacher. As Fraiberg says, "Behind the uncritical adulation for the father were the passive longings for the father, and these had eluded analysis throughout."[8]

I believe Eric was homosexual, because his history is similar to that described by gay adolescents and adults I have seen over the past thirty years. And if he was homosexual, then I view the increased conflict about his sexual orientation as a poor treatment outcome that in all likelihood served to reinforce a belief that his sexual feelings were perverse, to aggravate his already poor self-esteem, to delay the discovery of his sexual orientation, and to decrease the chance that he would be able to establish passionate, long-lasting attachments in later life. His poor self-regard would also increase the likelihood that he would engage in unsafe sexual encounters (see Chapter 5).

Adolescence is a tumultuous period for heterosexuals and homosexuals alike because there is instability of skills and interests and of defenses and character traits. But uncertainty about sexual identity is more characteristic of the homosexual adolescent than the heterosexual. As I discuss later, whereas heterosexual adolescents may have occasional homoerotic impulses and fantasies, they enter adolescence believing they are heterosexual and generally remain convinced of this.

Homosexual boys usually enter adolescence hoping that they are heterosexual, and it is only during late adolescence or early adulthood that they are able to acknowledge their sexual orientation. Because of the anxiety connected with their uncertainty about sexual identity, psychotherapeutic intervention, as trying and difficult as it is with any adolescent, can make large differences and be very rewarding. The resolution of uncertainty about and the beginning of consolidation of their sexual orientation can lead to self-esteem enhancement and a significant decrease in anxiety and depression.

I first saw Paul when he was a nineteen-year-old college junior. I worked with him for eight years, initially seeing him three times a week in psychoanalysis and then in twice-weekly analytic therapy. He had been seeing another analyst since his junior year in high school, but left because he was feeling increasingly depressed and hopeless about ever being able to live a happy life. He feared that he was homosexual because he was turned on by other boys. His sexual fantasies, for as long as he could remember, had been almost exclusively about boys. He hated his homosexuality and wanted desperately to be heterosexual. He was distressed by the way he met other boys, which was in the rest room of his college library. He labeled himself alternately "a sissy," "sick," "sleazy," or "disgusting."

In his first session he informed me that he thought his mother would be devastated if he were homosexual. He wanted to be straight for her, to live a conventional life, to give her the grandchildren that she so often said she wanted. It was she who urged him to go into therapy at age fifteen because of his lack of aggressiveness, which made her believe he might be homosexual.

Paul gave me the impression that his mother, chronically lacking energy and enthusiasm, had been moderately depressed during his childhood. He also described her as having often been irritated with and dismissive of his father. At the time of his brother's birth, she turned away from him to the new child, possibly because of depression and marital difficulties that left her with little resilience or energy to care for two children. From that time he believed that to please her he had to be good, get good grades, and be popular. She was never able to make Paul feel that he was unconditionally regarded, respected, or loved.

His father preferred the brother, two years younger, who was more masculine-appearing, more outgoing, and more athletic. John occupied a lot of his father's as well as his mother's time and attention because he was the more demanding child. Paul felt that for all these reasons he had been neglected by his father. Both his mother's inability to nurture Paul's self-regard and his father's rejection contributed to Paul's low self-esteem, making it difficult for him to accept that he was homosexual.

It was easy for Paul to be closer to girls than to boys. He had warmer friendships with them, as do many gay male adolescents and adults who feel that they have more in common with girls than with their conventionally masculine peers.

Although Paul experienced little attraction to girls, in order to please his peers and his mother he occasionally dated and attempted to have sex. The sex was passionless and, therefore, not satisfying. In fact, it was a source of despair, since it made him uncertain that he had the capacity to fall in love. Because he believed that his own needs and desires were unimportant to his parents, his attempts at heterosexual sex were also accompanied by a great deal of rage, which contributed to his distress.

I formed an early impression that Paul was homosexual because of his longstanding exclusively homoerotic fantasy life and his conscious desire for men. I viewed his rejection of his homosexuality and his desire to be heterosexual as symptoms of his injured self-esteem.

Whenever Paul had an anonymous sexual encounter in the rest room of his college library, he would spend hours admonishing himself for engaging in behavior that he believed despicable. At the beginning of his treatment, he could express his sexuality only in these encounters that he felt were sleazy. He did not think a romantic or lasting relationship was possible.

Anonymous or random sexual encounters are not necessarily a symptom of an inability to form intimate attachments. Peer and parental pressure for heterosexual conformity, our society's unwillingness to permit gay youth to develop a system of courtship, and the ease with which two men can get off with each other contribute to the need of some adolescents and adults to express their sexuality covertly. Rest rooms, pornographic movie theaters, bookstores, and the Internet may also provide an opportunity to meet and talk with others like themselves.

I often inquired, therefore, why Paul could not get more

pleasure from these available outlets for sexual contact. These questions implicitly acknowledged to him that I affirmed his need to express his sexuality, an attitude that rapidly helped to improve his mood and sense of well-being. It was a first but important step in helping him find more gratification in his sexual encounters, which led after about two years of therapy to his being able to acknowledge to himself that he was gay.

As Paul began to accept himself as homosexual, he also started to question why brief sexual encounters were his only source of sexual pleasure and why being close to another seemed difficult for him. He became more willing to meet men in school and through social activities without feeling self-conscious. This self-consciousness, which made him appear uninterested and detached, disguised his desire to reject other men as he had felt rejected by his father.

Just as the sexual anxiety of a heterosexual adolescent may evolve from repressed early erotic fantasies and desire for the mother, failures in intimacy of a gay adolescent like Paul may be caused by the repression and denial of the early erotic attachment to his father or an older relative. For some homosexual adolescents and adults, the recovery of these erotic memories may lead to rapid resolution of inhibitions in sexual functioning or in difficulties with intimate relations. Paul's early childhood, however, made the recovery of these memories difficult. His mother had deprecated his father, and Paul felt humiliated by his attachment to him. The withdrawal of both parents after John's birth and his father's preference for this younger sibling were added humiliations. For some time, therefore, Paul remembered his father only as a vague and unimportant person in his early life. Clearer memories emerged only after he could recall the pain, disappointment, and rejection he experienced from his father's withdrawal at the time of John's birth, as well as his intense rivalry with his brother. Then there was a gradual emergence of longing for the father and some vague recollection of early sexual feelings for him.

As in any dynamic therapy, Paul's thoughts about me in the transference were important to his understanding of his early relationships, particularly his relationship with his father. At first Paul appeared detached to the point of not having any feelings at all about me. He seemed to be oblivious of my appearance, habits, any interruptions or vacations—anything that one might expect to be noted by a patient, even early in his therapy.

During the first two years I frequently commented on his need to ignore me, wondering whether it wasn't protecting him from uncomfortable feelings. I was certain that my experience of being ignored by him reflected his wish to reject other men as he had been rejected. Gradually Paul was able to acknowledge that occasionally I made him feel rejected and angry, particularly if I was late starting an hour. Around the end of the fourth year of his analysis he had a dream about me:

> I meet this guy; he's selling me something. I am in a cave or a dark environment. I really feel like sleeping with him, but I don't know if he's gay. He looks very conventional; he has long, nonstyled hair. He's tall and skinny, almost like Tarzan. His pants are open. He's wearing a bathing suit underneath. I reach out and grab his leg. We start making out. I say something like, "Let's take off our clothes and let me suck your dick." I suck his cock and then I sit on it. It feels great. Then I remember his coming; just this wonderful feeling.

I needed to say little about the dream. Paul quickly understood that the dream had to do with me.

Over the next several months there was a notable lack of any further mention of similar erotic feelings. He pointedly emphasized that he was only interested in boys younger than he, those who had a childlike, blond, slight, and slender appearance. This attraction had two main determinants: an erotic interest in the younger brother, John, which was a displacement from his father, and an undoing of his aggression toward the brother. Boys of slight and slender appearance were also different both from his father and from me. On two or three occasions he had one-night encounters with men in their mid-forties, which belied his professed interest only in younger boys.

In his sixth year of treatment, Paul, who was then about twenty-five, dreamed: "I'm in a room; it looks like a cell. Some guy comes up after me, breathing heavily. I back up from him, digging my heels into the floor, going backwards." He commented that if he backed up he would back into me, since he was lying on the couch. And then he asserted: "I can't have feelings for anyone. . . . I am tired of therapy and tired of the silent bit on your part."

Paul again began to speak about his father's attention to his younger brother. John was having severe emotional difficulties that required his father to spend a lot of time with him and help him financially, which made Paul even more aware of his jealousy. He dreamed during this period: "John was in a serious auto accident. I told my father. He didn't seem upset."

Paul spoke of how furious he was at his father for lending his brother his car. I interpreted the murderous rage expressed in his dream. Then he recalled memories of his father's spending time with John when they were children and how much he had resented this. For the first time he told me how badly he had wanted his father to spend time alone with him. In subsequent hours he returned to the theme of longing for his father, often obscured by his competitiveness with and jealousy of John. He complained about my not saying enough or giving him enough advice. If he was going to get what he wanted and what he needed, he believed, he had to cheat or steal.

Then, once again, there was an emergence of erotic feelings in his dreams:

> I'm in a bathroom trying to piss into the urinal. Some of the piss gets on me. I go into a locker room to change. There is a kid, maybe fifteen or sixteen. I stick my dick in front of him. He touches it and says, "I really like this dick." He says, "I can't believe I'm saying that." There are people around and I said to him, "We can't stay here."

Paul recognizes that "Dick" is my name and says, as he said in the dream, "I can't believe I'm saying that." He recalled showering with his father many times, both at home and in locker rooms, and looking at his penis. He could not remember this as being exciting or his father's penis as looking attractive.

His dreams and associations then became more explicitly sexual, as did his wanting me to notice him and to be attracted to him: "I'm on the couch, lying on my stomach. I have an erection and turn around to look up and talk to you." He sees both his father and me as being distant, and this angers him.

Over the subsequent weeks another theme emerged: his wish to be passive and submissive. The longing to be submissive in relation to other men expressed his desire to feel connected to his distant father and to me by being sexually penetrated. He viewed his wish to be penetrated as being womanlike, which filled him with anxiety and disgust:

> I'm in a swimming pool. There is all kinds of shit in there. There's a bundle all tied together. I put it under the

water and it freezes. A large tractor-trailer drives into the pool. It moves back and forth to get out. As it goes back and forth there's a fire at one end of the pool. There's a guy there in danger of being injured.

He describes the guy in the dream as being in his forties. He reminds him of Rudy Giuliani, then a federal prosecutor. He thinks of me and his father. He wonders whether I am gay or straight. "I want you to be straight and not gay. I'd be more uptight here if you were gay. Giuliani is straight like you." At this point in his analysis he needs to see me as being straight to protect himself from erotic feelings for me and for his father, feelings that terrify him.

I told Paul I was gay the following year, after he was able to ask me. As I discussed in the previous chapter, knowledge of my sexual orientation did not alter the nature of the transference. My being a gay man whom he regarded highly did help to consolidate a view of himself as a worthwhile person who was also homosexual.

The importance of Paul's feelings for me in the transference in helping him gain access to his early erotic feelings for his father cannot be overestimated. It was in the immediacy of his relationship with me that he was able to reexperience his earliest fantasies toward his father, which had heretofore been repressed. Furthermore, Paul gradually became more and more capable of experiencing warmth and affection both from and for me. This helped make it possible for him to have both sexual and affectionate feelings for the young men that he was meeting.

During the last two years of our work, Paul, then in his late twenties, had several brief relationships. We had many opportunities to explore how his rage at his father and his disgust over the nature of his passive sexual longings led him to reject those who liked him, and attracted him to those who were least interested. Random sexual encounters outside of a relationship became less and less satisfying as a means of contact and sexual release.

As Paul felt more lovable and less dependent on peers for acceptance, he cautiously began to let others know that he was gay. He came out to his parents and was surprised to find that his father was particularly accepting of him. Although his mother was initially angry and hurt, over the subsequent year or two she also was able to begin to accept this aspect of him and his life.

Paul decided to stop treatment after eight years. He was beginning a relationship with Ben. Paul was very much in love, and this helped him further consolidate his sexuality and integrate it into an increasingly firm and good sense of himself. We both believed that he now knew himself well enough to be able to work without me on any difficulties that might arise.

About six months after we finished, he wrote me about some outstanding problems that still troubled him, but he felt he was dealing with them adequately. He concluded, "For the first time in my life I am happy, and it is because of Ben and the knowledge that he is out there for me. It is a feeling that I don't ever want to live without."

Properly conducted therapy helps the homosexual adolescent consolidate his sexuality by removing impediments that may have interfered with his acknowledging his sexual orientation; particularly, the negative self-perceptions that have evolved from self-esteem injury due to the empathic failure of their parents or their outright rejection, later peer rejection, and social stigmatization. At the close of adolescence, by twenty, twenty-one, or twenty-two years, the homosexual youth should have the capacity to accept a variety of homo-erotic fantasies, to be able to fall in and out of love without too great disruption of his life, and to enjoy sex with other men. With positive self-regard, he will value his own health and be mindful of the health of his partners. Like the heterosexual adolescent, he should ideally be able to experience himself as a loving, sexual person.[9]

Homosexual Fantasies and Impulses in Heterosexual Adolescents

Homosexual impulses and fantasies occur in heterosexual adolescents for three main reasons. First, they may arise out of fear of retaliation from emerging heterosexual prowess and competitive strivings. Second, homosexual feelings may occur because of a real or imagined unavailability of a girl or from injury to self-esteem due to rejection by a girl. They may also emerge if the heterosexual adolescent becomes frightened of being drawn back into a childlike dependency on his mother. Adolescent boys who are so frightened by their dependency are likely to have had mothers whom they long for because they had been emotionally or physically absent or who were engulfing and engendered inadequate boundaries. Even an adolescent with more normal parenting may struggle against urges to be dependent on his mother by mentally revisiting his childhood attachment to his father, which may evoke homosexual fantasies or impulses.[10]

When homosexual impulses occur in a heterosexual adolescent, they usually are not manifest in behavior, but if they are, the sex is occasional, playful, without passion, and usually anxiety-ridden.

Heterosexual adolescents, even if they have conflicts caused by their dependency, competitiveness, or early maternal relationship and have experimented with homosexual sex, have fantasies that remain predominantly heterosexual and seek out girls without urging or coercion. There is too much heterosexual drive and pressure for peer acceptance and conformity to sustain sexual interest in other boys. It is only the gay adolescent with his persistent homosexual fantasies and impulses, and who also has strong, positive self-regard, who will be able to maintain homosexual activity during this developmental stage.[11]

For the healthy development of both homosexual and heterosexual adolescents in treatment, the clinician must be clear about the distinctions between the gay adolescent and the heterosexual who has homosexual feelings. The following case illustrates how a heterosexual adolescent with such impulses may appear.

Tom was a nineteen-year-old college sophomore referred to me because of his longstanding troublesome depression and severe anxiety, the latter often occurring when he was in bed at night. He had briefly seen another therapist, whom he had found unempathic and occasionally unkind.

He was the only child of a father described as demanding, strict, and controlling and a mother who was perceived as unaffectionate and distant. Tom was an intelligent, perceptive, extremely anxious young man whose anxiety was in part related to his desire to be controlled by a man like his father and to his competitive feelings toward him. He had occasional homosexual masturbation fantasies that troubled him, although most of his fantasies, both masturbation and daydreams, were heterosexual.

In the early part of his analysis, he had some dreams with explicit homoerotic content, such as this one in his first year: "I'm in a room with Betsy. Suddenly I get the urge to suck my friend off. I have his penis in my mouth." His associations were to his previous impotence with a girlfriend and to a scene in the movie *Midnight Cowboy* where a man "shoves the phone down the throat of this homosexual." Occasionally, he said, he would walk by a particular janitor and fantasize that the janitor would "shove a broom up my ass." His homosexual dreams and fantasies expressed his anger toward his controlling father and his longing for him, especially when he was rebuffed by a girl. In his associations to this dream, he recalled crawling into bed with his father and his father's playfully shoving his tongue in his ear.

Another dream from the same period of analysis was: "You are standing in the door of the bathroom. There are white tiles in it. You look about fifteen feet tall." He remembered seeing his father's penis when he was a child. He sees a good-looking guy and thinks of putting a penis in his mouth. It "makes my stomach get tight."

Approaching the summer before his senior year in college and the last year of his three-year analysis, Tom was eager to get away from treatment. He felt there were better job opportunities out of the city. He also knew that he was anxious about feeling too close and was eager to get away from me. "I hate the idea of being tied to this. . . . I hate the idea that you have other patients. I saw one the other day and I felt like going for his throat. Every time I come in here, I feel I just get squeezed in."

I commented on how furious he got when he felt close to me and how his anger was related to his anger at his father. In response he said:

> I loved my father when I was a kid. He was more gentle than my mother, and more around too . . . more playful. A minute ago you said something very softly. I felt like putting my hand on your shoulder. I feel like getting off the couch. When I was talking about how playful my father was, I felt like opening my mouth and putting your penis inside.

> Sometimes at night now I get this peaceful feeling, like I have a big watermelon in my mouth.

Tom's strong attachment to his father appeared to be an attempt to get the gratification that he did not obtain from his emotionally inhibited mother, whom he perceived as distant, uninvolved, uncaring, and incompetent.[12] His homosexual fantasies and feelings made him "feminine," which caused him to have less desire for his mother and feel less competitive with his father and, thereby, less endangered.

As erotic desire for his mother became less repressed and more tolerable, his heterosexual fantasies became less inhibited and his relationships with girls improved. Homosexual fantasies that had been precipitated by the absence of sexual partners or by feeling rejected by them or by his anxiety over his heterosexuality abated.

I received a letter from Tom about four years after he finished his analysis. He had resolved some vocational issues and was now planning to go to graduate school. He was engaged to marry a girl he had met at college during the last year of his analysis.

Developmental Tasks

The homosexual adolescent's self-acknowledgment is, for him, the most important developmental task of this stage of his life, beginning the consolidation and integration of his sexual orientation. It is the first stage in his becoming gay. Ideally, his sexuality will become positively integrated, a process made difficult for many because of early paternal rejection, later peer rejection, the internalization of society's prejudice, and the paucity of good role models.[13]

One might reasonably assume that, like the heterosexual, the young adolescent of twelve or thirteen, with the upsurge of his sexual impulses at the time of physiological maturation, would be able to recognize his homosexuality. But we have seen the many reasons for delays in this process, particularly his injured self-esteem; therefore, it is not until eighteen, nineteen, or even later that the majority of homosexual adolescents are able to acknowledge their sexual orientation to themselves.[14]

The adolescent who is able to self-acknowledge has to be relatively free of self-esteem impairment in order to overcome the denial of his same-sex feelings, caused by the lack of his parents' empathy with his difference from other boys, paternal rejection, later peer rejection, fear of disappointing his parents, social stigmatization, negative stereotypes, and the absence of role models. To self-acknowledge he must also have achieved enough independence and self-reliance to realize that he is never going to be able to fulfill those needs of his parents that relate to his living a conventional life with a conventional family. To some extent he has to give up his wish to do so. Self-acknowledgment often occurs only after the boy has fallen in love, a passion powerful enough to help overcome his denial.

Extensive sexual fantasies with masturbation are as important in consolidating the sexuality of the homosexual adolescent as they are for the heterosexual. Sexual experimentation within an affectionate relationship is more likely to lead to the beginning of positive integration than are sexual encounters that are anonymous. However, such relationships are not as available to gay youth as to heterosexual adolescents who are exploring their sexuality.

Coming out to other gay adolescents and adults, or homosocialization, helps him overcome the despair that is often caused by feeling stigmatized and rejected by peers or family. It provides him with an antidote to his sense of cognitive and social isolation and is a refuge from the verbal and physical abuse to which many are subjected, particularly those least conventional in appearance and behavior.[15] Friendships with other gay adolescents and involvement in gay social networks provide alliances, sexual partners, and role models whom they may idealize and with whom they may identify.

Some of those with whom gay youth identify and who are seen as adult role models are also HIV positive or have AIDS, making the possibility of acquiring HIV seem likely or even desirable as a means of solidifying their identification with the gay community. It is essential that we find ways to stress the importance of living a long, happy, and healthy life by providing HIV-negative role models who are in long-term, committed relationships without undermining the value and worth either of those who are HIV positive or the pleasure of sex.[16]

Fear of parental rejection is often strong in gay adolescents. Coming out to parents, therefore, does not usually occur until late adolescence or early adulthood and often follows coming out to other gay youths, some sexual experimentation, and, frequently, the confirming and powerful experience of falling in love.

All adolescents need to detach from their parents to counter anxiety about their continued wishes to be dependent, to foster greater self-reliance, and to test capabilities in a widening social sphere. Coming out to his parents can serve these developmental needs for the homosexual adolescent, who in this way proclaims his difference from them and, thus, his independence. When the parental response is appropriately accepting, the adolescent is reassured of his parents' love and support not only as a homosexual person but as a person who is separate from them, both of which contribute to the likelihood that he will integrate his sexual orientation in a positive way.

Parents who angrily reject their child for being gay are likely to have always required that he meet their needs and expectations and have offered little support or respect for the development of his independence, individuality, and self-reliance. When an adolescent in these families finally does acknowledge his sexual orientation to his parents, he frequently does so with an angry defiance that is intended to injure them, thereby providing him with enough space from parental expectations to enable his further growth and self-reliance.

I have had the opportunity to see many parents whose adolescent boys have acknowledged their homosexuality during middle to late adolescence (seventeen to twenty-one or twenty-two years of age). The parents are often distressed because they may not have grandchildren, or by the hardship they see for their child, or because of displaced guilt. But the parents who seek me out are usually respectful of their child's difference and seek consultation to overcome their own concerns so they can provide a loving and accepting family environment.[17]

When I have seen the adolescent children of parents who are concerned about providing a loving and accepting environment, they have a positive self-regard unusual for any adolescent, which helps them to contend with the peer stigmatization and prejudice they are inevitably encountering with appropriate anger but without a need to abuse alcohol or other drugs and without masochistic, depressive, or other disabling neurotic character defenses.

It often happens that when there is a need to cope with unplanned or unexpected events, latent capacities and abilities to cope become apparent. This always occurs when a homosexual adolescent or young adult self-acknowledges. He has to find ways to express his sexuality within a prejudiced society and to deal with his heterosexual peers. He begins to think about his differences from his family of origin as well as his peers. Questions arise in his mind about his future and the choices he will have to make, including the possible relinquishment of previous expectations about living a conventional life and having his own family.

For all adolescents, the testing of social limits, reckless and even at times dangerous behavior, and the seeking out of relationships that trouble parents express the wish to have external social forces intervene to help counter internal sexual and aggressive pressures that are frightening because they are new and painful. By pitting their impulses against the demands and expectations of parents and society, all adolescents expand their ability to contain, control, organize, and cope with a variety of new situations.[18]

Although there are limits to the possibilities of growth in any person's life, the ambiguity of his social role and, with this ambiguity, the freedom he has to define his role, give the gay adolescent more occasions than his heterosexual peers to test and expand his skills in coping with and mastering new and often problematic circumstances and relationships. The gay adolescent who self-acknowledges has opportunities to plan his life to a large extent without being constrained by convention and social expectations. With these opportunities comes the freedom as well as the burden of determining his own future.

4 The Dilemma of Heterosexually Married Homosexual Men

All that is left is to pretend. But to pretend to the end of one's life is the highest torment.

—PETER TCHAIKOVSKY after his marriage in 1877

Given the inability of many homosexual men to accept their sexual orientation, and their need to conform to society's expectation, some have pursued heterosexual marriages.[1] I have seen fourteen homosexual men in consultation who have been married to women, and I have worked in therapy for one year or longer with nine of them. Seven of the nine divorced, five while in treatment and two before starting therapy. Two remain married.

Although divorce from a spouse of many years is always stressful, the decision to divorce made by a homosexual man is a particularly complex developmental step that may be psychologically perilous. This decision often involves moving from many years of denial of sexual orientation to self-acknowledgment and then to varying degrees of self-acceptance. The transition from heterosexual marriage to a gay relationship entails giving up the refulgent respectability provided by marriage. It usually also means public acknowledgment of being homosexual and coping with prejudice and stigmatization.

Most homosexual men marry because they are denying their homosexuality. Some know they are homosexual but choose to marry anyway for a variety of reasons. They may want to live a conventional, heterosexual life because of its relative ease, comfort, and social respectability. They may marry because of a desire to have children and the conviction that it is in the best interests of these children; they may wish to please parents. A homosexual man may also marry because he loves his future spouse. Since the early 1980s, some have married with the hope of avoiding infection with HIV.[2]

Whether he denies or is aware of his sexual orientation, any homosexual man who marries does so, in my clinical experience, because of early self-esteem injury that has caused him to see his homosexuality as bad, sinful, or sick. Being heterosexual, he feels, is better or healthier, and he has the unconscious expectation that with marriage will come the longed-for regard of others. Most hope that however powerful their homoerotic inclinations are or however compelling past sexual experiences have been, marriage will cure them.

Every married homosexual man I have seen has needed to repeat with his spouse the sense of having been emotionally deprived or disappointed by his mother. The futile hope of mastering this trauma provides one powerful but unconscious motive for these heterosexual marriages. During much of the marriage there is usually rage at the spouse as a maternal surrogate. Some conflict-ridden marriages of heterosexual men may, of course, have the same unconscious determinant. And it is always possible that there are gay men who do not seek help because they are in marriages without significant conflict; however, I believe a man's homosexuality will likely be a major source of conflict in a heterosexual marriage unless he has a strong bisexual component to his sexuality, as I discuss later.

Another motive, again unconscious, for the marriage of some homosexual men is their attempt to obtain the long-sought but elusive love and approval of a father by accepting the socially ascribed male role of husband and father. A number of the married homosexual men I have seen have been explicitly or implicitly encouraged to marry by analysts or analytically oriented therapists to help them overcome what the analyst views as inhibitions of his patient's heterosexuality. The wish to please a therapist by getting married usually derives from the frustrated desire to obtain a father's love. Improperly conducted psychoanalysis or therapy should be considered another reason some gay men marry.[3]

The advice of many therapists today resembles that given to André Gide one hundred years ago before his marriage. A "specialist of considerable renown," whom he consulted because of growing doubts and anxiety caused by his homosexuality, advised:

> "You say, however, that you are in love with a girl and that you are hesitating to marry her, knowing your tastes on the other hand. . . . Get married. Get married without fear. And you will soon see that all the rest exists only in your imagination. You remind me of a starving man who has been trying until now to exist on pickles!" (I am quoting his words exactly; heaven knows, I remember them well enough!) "As for the natural instinct, you won't be married long before you realize what it is and return to it spontaneously."

Gide goes on to say:

> What I soon realized, on the contrary, was how wrong the theoretician was. He was wrong like all those who insist upon considering homosexual tastes . . . as acquired tendencies and therefore modifiable through upbringing, promiscuities, love. . . . Love exalted me, to be sure, but, despite what the doctor had predicted, it in no wise brought about through marriage a normalization of my desires. At most, it got me to observe chastity, in a costly effort that served merely to split me further. Heart and senses pulled me in opposite directions.[4]

During the first year or two, most homosexual men are able to have sex with their wives, albeit without much passion. They are enthralled by the excitement or exaltation of being married. They enjoy the conventionality, social acceptance, and approval of parents. Homosexual men usually want children, and they make responsible, caring fathers—in part, because they are relatively more comfortable with the nurturing aspects of their personality than are heterosexual men. Their capacity to be good fathers often enhances the loving bond between husband and wife as well as between the homosexual father and his children.

Most homosexual men describe feeling increasingly anxious or depressed after the first few years of marriage. Sex is by then experienced as work and is approached with anxiety. Since heterosexual sex for a homosexual man usually has procreation and not pleasure as a goal, it typically decreases in frequency or ceases altogether after the birth of the first child.

Those men who stop having sex with other men in anticipation of marriage usually resume after the first few years. Initially it is anonymous and often takes place in public rest rooms, gay-oriented pornographic movies, or with male escorts where it can be quick and unintrusive.[5] Internet hook-ups are also now a way to meet for quick and, usually, anonymous sex. Over the ensuing years these random encounters are found to be increasingly unsatisfying because of the desire for a loving attachment to another man.

It is interesting that separation or divorce so frequently occurs after fifteen to twenty-five years. The gay man is by then either in a close relationship with another man or longs for one. The children are more independent and now no longer need the same amount of attention; often they are out of the home. Both husband and wife feel a growing sense of distance, isolation, loneliness, and despair.

When these marriages break up, they usually do so not out of lack of love, affection, or mutual respect but because either partner has a need to make a life that is more fulfilling and consonant with his or her inherent longings and desires. But not all homosexual men want to leave their wives. Commitment and attachment, guilt over their anger, and ambivalence about their sexual orientation may all contribute to a decision to remain married.

A few years ago I received a long letter from a man in his late forties who had been married for more than twenty years. His history and despair are shared by many homosexual men who remain in their marriages:

> My sexual thoughts and interests are almost always of the same sex. I have been aware of this feeling since I was four years old. I remember when an older cousin came to our farm when I was four. He rode in on a motorcycle, in a leather jacket, hat and gloves, and his shirt was open. Dark, black, curly hair showed out of the top and I remember

being very excited seeing it, and still remember that scene some forty years later. I remember to my shock and surprise what other men and boys looked like when I first went to a public swimming pool in our town. I was very excited at their size and by the hair that grew on that part of the body and enjoyed very much going to the pool because of this. I had never seen a man undressed before and probably spent a good deal of time staring at other men. I knew that I enjoyed being there, and expressed that to my long-time pal that I had been with since I was about four.

My first sexual experience was an accidental self-induced one while taking a bath. I discovered . . . how good it felt to scrub my penis and continued to do this until I had this awesome feeling and white liquid came out of it. I was frightened and did not know what I had done, but knew that it felt good. This was about age twelve. I discovered it with my pal and he told me that it was "coming," and that it was semen and that nothing bad had happened. A short time later, he asked me if I had ever played "cow." He had me assume a position on hands and knees and proceeded to take my pants down and stroke my now rigid penis. It felt extremely good and I then had him do the same thing. This was the first time I had ever touched another man's penis. It was a wonderful feeling. We began doing this fairly regularly. Quite often, we would mount each other missionary position and he told me that was how men and women made love. We were probably sixteen before we sucked each other's penises, an act that I was at first as frightened of doing as he was. In the times that we did, we never came in each other's mouths—it seemed disgusting at that time. Our on- and off-masturbation lasted until I left home when I was seventeen. We are still friends to this day, but we have never discussed it between ourselves.

As time went along, I had other mutual masturbation sessions with first a dock boy and then a close friend at my high school, which all led to oral sex. I did long many times to have a friend, which I thought should be a girl. I did not have any understanding of homosexuality, nor would I have even accepted that that was a direction in which I was headed. My sex with the few guys was justified as just "helping each other out."

When I was eighteen another friend and I had sex together. He was about twenty-eight at the time. He was the one and only person who ejaculated in my mouth. It was a shock to me and I felt deeply ashamed. I went home and cried and was so ashamed of my life at that time that I contemplated suicide. I even tape-recorded messages to my family. The sorrow passed somewhat. I continued on but never saw him again. He left a deep mark on me, and the shame continued for years.

My growing up was very painful as I realized that I was somehow different from other boys my age. I knew that I didn't enjoy the same feelings for girls that other guys described. I dated usually for periods of time with the same girl, which I now know was probably a safety thing. Kissing was okay but never caused me to become erect or excited. My first experience with a woman was with a prostitute that a friend in school encouraged me to see with him. That experience was not fulfilling and was hard to complete.

In my twenties I strongly felt a need to find a regular girlfriend. I dated one for six years and had regular intercourse with her, which consisted of simply getting myself off without really considering what her needs were. I did not understand what any woman's needs were. During the time that I was dating this girl, I continued to have sex occasionally with men when the opportunity arose, but, again, only with people I knew and not promiscuously. One was a roommate who encouraged me while he pretended to be asleep. This was an eight-month experience until he got married.

In my twenty-sixth year, I met a very wonderful girl who was a constant encouragement to me, and we became engaged a month after we met. I was very excited by her and we began first having sex about three months after we met. We married within ten months and out of this marriage we had two nice children. As time went on, it became harder and harder to have satisfactory sexual relations with her and many times it was accomplished only by the sheer friction that would make me in an aroused state. As the years have gone on, it has become more and more difficult to have relations with her, even though my feelings have not diminished and we still get along very well.

My feelings for other men have not diminished. My dreams are all still homosexual, although my actions, for the most part, are not. I continue to enjoy the sight, smell, and touch of other men, and see many of them at my health club. All of them are heterosexual, and I prefer my friends to be that way, I guess, because I have never had a close friend that I could be sexual with and still keep as a friend. Although I know a lot of gay men as acquaintances, I feel very uncomfortable around them and do not socialize with them at the present time.

It has been some years since my last sexual experience with a man, but that hasn't reduced the longing to be with one, to be held closely, and to be told that he loves me. I have two [straight] friends who I am close to, who hug me often and express that they love me, but I could never express to them what I truly feel and constantly keep on my guard with them. It's hard to explain the ache that one has and the longing to be close to another man.

> I know that I did not pursue the orientation that I have, and know that I have always been as I am now. I know that it becomes more difficult to live in the lonely shell that I do now, but can see no way out of it.

Like most homosexual men who have been married for many years, he experiences little or no sexual passion for his wife or other women and desires a sexual and emotional connection to a man. But also, like many, he loves his wife and his children. He sees no way out of the conflict he experiences between his desire to love and be loved by another man and his devotion to his family. In order to remain in his marriage, he has not had sex with a man for some years. His insight into the inherent frustration of his complex situation and his capacity to verbalize and tolerate this frustration have probably helped him to remain in his marriage, albeit with despair and loneliness.

Middle age brings an increased awareness of the finitude of life. With this awareness comes the enhanced desire, before it's too late, to repair discontinuities between one's needs, wishes, and ambitions and longstanding social responsibilities and expectations. Perhaps we are then better equipped, because of previous experience resolving conflict, to confront heretofore repressed or denied needs and wishes and to tolerate the losses sustained by the expression of these needs. Therapists are often sought at this developmental stage, and they may be helpful in resolving this difficult crisis of middle adulthood.[6]

Peter

Peter came to me for help with his depression. He was forty-six and had been married for about twenty years when I first started to work with him. He had not had sex with his wife for about fifteen years, had no homosexual experiences since his marriage, and wanted to remain married. He had no interest in becoming gay.

Peter had a history of moderately heavy drinking for which he had seen a therapist when he was about forty. The therapist had been helpful with this problem but not with his lack of sexual interest in his wife. He had attempted to talk about his longstanding attraction to men, but his psychiatrist viewed homosexuality as a defense against heterosexual impulses and gave little credence to Peter's fear that he was homosexual. Therapy was terminated because the therapist believed that Peter was not motivated to discuss his marital difficulties.

He came to see me about two years later, desiring relief from his depression and alcohol intake, both of which had increased over the past year. He wanted to understand why he was so lonely and to improve communication with his wife.

He believed the lack of sex with his wife had caused considerable tension but found it difficult to discuss any problematic issues with her because he feared confrontation and anger—his own as well as others'. He thought he would also find it difficult to discuss his homosexuality with me, believing that, if he did, he would want to "become gay." He needed the conventionality offered by his wife, child, and upper middle class life, he told me, in order to continue to be professionally successful.

A few weeks after his initial consultation, Peter hesitantly began to speak about his homosexual activity as an adolescent and the few experiences he had had in his early twenties. His sexual contacts had always been followed by disgust and guilt.

He had first sought psychological help, he told me, in his mid-twenties because of concern about his sexual impulses, telling his therapist that he wanted to live a normal life, to marry and have children. According to Peter, the therapist had responded that he should put homosexual thoughts out of his mind and start to date women. Shortly thereafter he met his future wife. They became engaged within a year and soon began to have sex, his first attempt at heterosexual sex. He found it passionless and mechanical, was often unable to get an erection, or ejaculated immediately upon penetration. His fiancée threatened to break off the engagement because of his sexual difficulties and lack of interest, prompting him to resume therapy.

Peter's interest in sex decreased further after they were married, and it ceased altogether after their only child was born. Although he cared about this child, he felt increasingly isolated from his wife and soon grew despondent about the state of his marriage. He felt lonely and empty. Work was the only area of his life that he considered successful.

Near the end of his first year of therapy, Peter spoke with me about his homosexual masturbation fantasies. The idea of a relationship with a man was unacceptable because it would threaten the conventional appearance of his life. Furthermore, having felt unloved and unappreciated by his father, who favored his more aggressive and athletic older brother, he now feared rejection whenever he experienced affection for or from another man.

Peter was detached and uninvolved in his relationship with me. He treated me and others as he had been treated by his parents; his detachment protected him from relationships that he was certain would inevitably be disappointing. Over time, with insight into the nature of the transference, he became more trusting and able to tolerate some dependence and affectionate feelings.

During five years of twice-weekly therapy, Peter grew more tolerant of his homosexual fantasies. He was able to masturbate with more comfort and greater frequency to homosexual images and even permitted himself surreptitious glances at an attractive man on the street or at gay pornography. The more in touch he was with his internal life, the less isolated and lonely he felt in all his relationships, especially with his wife.

As our work progressed and Peter understood his frustrated longing to be loved and acknowledged by his parents, he became less dependent on the recognition of his colleagues. By the end of therapy his depression had lessened and he no longer drank. He was in touch with his homosexual desire and felt less empty, although his sexual pleasure remained limited to masturbation with homosexual fantasies and occasional glances at gay magazines. He did not speak with his wife about his sexual orientation or about their sexual difficulties, since, as he often exclaimed, "I don't discuss anything with her anyway." As he became less critical of himself, though, he grew more tolerant of others, more productive at work, more respectful of his wife, and, generally, more loving.

Peter had married because he hated his homosexuality. Injured self-esteem had made it impossible to accept homosexual feelings that might alienate his parents or peers. He needed to appear conventional in a futile attempt to win the love, praise, and admiration of both parents, especially his father. He repeated with his wife the profound sense of rejection experienced from his self-involved mother. He remained married, not only because he obtained gratification from his marriage and felt committed to his wife and child, but also because of his need to repeat and master the feeling of emotional deprivation he had experienced with his parents.

Peter will always suffer from a degree of depression and have to deal with his loneliness and a sense of isolation, but, like the writer of the previous letter, he remains reasonably content.

John

John was in his early forties when he came to see me, unhappy and contemplating divorce. He believed his marriage was hindering his efforts to deal with his homosexuality, and he wanted to "become more gay." Like Peter, he had been married for about twenty years; unlike Peter, he wanted out of his marriage.

John had been in therapy for many years with a psychoanalyst who, he believed, had been critical of him and viewed his homosexuality as an emotional disturbance. He hoped that I would be less biased.

During his childhood, neither his mother nor his father were affectionate with their children. John, like Peter, described his mother as selfish and his father as perfectionistic, demanding, ambitious, and unavailable. He worked hard in school to please his parents, hard enough to be admitted to an Ivy League college. In spite of the ebullience, intelligence, and energy that made him popular, he had felt isolated, lonely, and unlovable.

John had been having casual sex with men since his last two years of high school, and in his third year of college he began a year-long affair with his roommate. He was comfortable while the relationship remained only sexual, but toward the end of the school year John began to feel that he was falling in love. He grew increasingly agitated and depressed, lost his appetite, and was unable to sleep. Anxiety interfered with his ability to study for finals, and wanting to get away from his lover, he left college. To avoid angering his father, John concocted a story about taking time off in order to prepare himself academically for his senior year.

He worked during the next year and then applied to and was accepted at a prestigious university, where he finished his senior year and subsequently began his postgraduate education. He started treatment with his first therapist during his last year of college in order to eradicate the homosexuality that he believed was causing his depression. Fearing criticism, he did not tell his therapist that he frequently cruised the rest rooms of his college library and the streets near the university to find sexual partners.

He met his future wife in graduate school. Although for as long as he could recall his sexual fantasies had been homosexual, he described sex with her as initially quite enjoyable. But he also continued to have frequent anonymous homosexual sex. His therapist encouraged his relationship with her, hoping thereby to eradicate the homosexuality. John married as he was nearing completion of graduate school.

Within the first two years, sex became occasional, passionless, and mechanical. He began to go to the baths once a week, although he went during work and not in the evening so that these interludes would not disrupt his home life. In order to feel detached during his sexual encounters and not to form any entanglements, he disguised his identity, giving his partners a false name, occupation, and phone number.

John felt ashamed of being homosexual, focusing his shame on the "sleaziness" and anonymity of his encounters. Seven or eight years after marrying, he began to desire more intimate relationships. One year before consulting me, he started to go to the baths several times a week, and a few months later he had met a man there with whom he believed he was falling in love. Before our first appointment, he was contemplating moving out of his house, although he had never told his wife of his homosexual encounters and was still totally closeted within his profession. Except for his new lover and one gay friend, he had told no one of his homosexuality.

John was proud of his fine home and the warm and loving

atmosphere he had created for his wife and children. He recognized that he needed the emotional security and comfort they provided. Therefore, I was concerned about his impulsive desire to leave them and his denial of the pain he might experience or social rejection he would encounter. Since for many years John had been distressed by his homosexuality and treated his sexual orientation as an unwanted habit that should be extricated, I believed the urgency of his wish to "become more gay" was due at least as much to his anxiety and shame about being homosexual as it was to his need for self-acceptance.

On the basis of his longstanding and nearly exclusive homosexual fantasies, I did feel that John was homosexual. I also believed that he had to acquire understanding of the unconscious rage that derived from the emotional deprivation of his childhood before his self-regard would be healthy enough that he could begin to consolidate and integrate his sexual orientation and form a positive sexual identity. Only then would he be able to deal with the stress of separation and divorce and be able to sustain a relationship with another man.

A few weeks after starting to see me, he rented an apartment so that he would have a place to spend time with his new lover. He told his wife he was working late, but when she called and found he was not at work, she became understandably suspicious. I mentioned that he was calling her attention to his affair in lieu of speaking with her because he was frightened by her anger. He needed time, I cautioned, to understand the motives behind his need to leave his family and his ambivalence about his homosexuality before pursuing this new relationship. My comments were met with disdain. Not wanting to be reminded of the conflict he felt about his sexual orientation, he suggested that I must be uncomfortable with my own homosexuality.

Five or six months after beginning therapy, John precipitously moved out of his home without explaining to his wife or children why he had done so. Although he returned regularly to take his children to school, his wife was shocked, bewildered, and furious.

His new lover did not move in with him, but they saw each other frequently. John told me that he now felt happy and free and denied any sadness or regret. But I was concerned that he had no social support and suggested he form some friendships with other gay men. He might begin to do so, I told him, by attending a group for gay men with children. He did take this advice, although he refused to use his correct name at the meetings. He had no plans to deal with his homosexuality with his professional colleagues, preferring to "take things one step at a time."

A few weeks after leaving home, he spoke with his wife, telling her that he had met a man and that he needed time to deal with the experience. He implied that this was his first homosexual experience, that it was probably a passing phase in his life, and that he was confused about his homosexual impulses.

It was shortly thereafter that his lover told John that he loved him. John then began to find him less attractive, to feel more detached, withdrawn, and closed in. Within a few weeks they were seeing each other less frequently and John broke off the relationship. His own increasing dependency and the sense of his lover's vulnerability had once again caused him to flee from an intimate relationship.

John returned home, ashamed and contrite. Because he was not sleeping well and appeared clinically depressed, I suggested that a trial of an antidepressant might stabilize his mood. He rejected the idea, fearing he might grow dependent on medication.

He told me how pleased he was to be back home, that he felt

comfortable, less depressed, and secure once again with his family. He particularly enjoyed spending time with his children, who were, of course, relieved that he had returned.

Two months later he again began to have occasional sex at the baths. Soon he was going to the baths several times a week. His relationship with his wife deteriorated when she became suspicious that he had resumed homosexual activity.

In therapy he spoke once again of his discontent and his desire to live as an openly gay man. He claimed to be comfortable with his homosexuality but also continued to express shame over his sexual encounters. He remained closeted in all aspects of his life, except for his one gay friend and the group, in which he had gradually begun to reveal more about himself. Because I continued to encourage him to find more gay friends and acquaintances on whom he could rely for support, John came out to another gay man whom he had known for many years. However, he soon became angry and disappointed with him for not being as attentive as he had hoped.

John had difficulty talking about the emotional deprivation of his childhood. I viewed his continued shame about sexual activity and the trouble he had forming friendships with gay men as symptoms of self-directed rage that were obstructing his ability to form a positive identity as a gay man. I also believed that the way he was attempting to cope with his marriage, flaunting his independence and his right to stay out late, was self-destructive. I interpreted his assertion of independence as having less to do with a need to express his sexuality, as he maintained, than with anger at his wife and children because of the impoverished and emotionally abusive relationship with both of his parents in his early childhood.

John now reluctantly agreed to start on an antidepressant, which, initially, helped to relieve his increasing agitation and depression, although not his sense of hopelessness. He stopped taking the medication abruptly and without discussion within one month because of its unpleasant side effects. He refused to try another.

Soon he met yet another man at the baths to whom he felt very attracted. Robert was HIV positive, demanding, very needy, and understandably anxious about his deteriorating health. He had an urgent need for an intimate relationship and wanted John to move in immediately. I could not think of a less appropriate lover for him at this time, since Robert became furious whenever John went home to be with his family.

I predicted that feeling dependent on Robert might eventually make him angry and then evoke guilt as it had in all previous intimate relationships. If he did leave home again and the relationship failed, I told him, his wife might not be willing to let him return. I pointed out that it would take time for him to understand his problem maintaining intimate relationships and that he should slow down. He mocked my concern.

John had been seeing me twice weekly for about a year and a half. He had worked hard in therapy but always had difficulty recalling details of the formative and traumatic relationship with his parents. He continued to make important decisions without discussing them with me. My inquiries about his not seeking guidance on these occasions always evoked the same response: "I have always done things on my own and am not about to change that now." When I tried to point out that his fear of feeling dependent and attached made it difficult to rely on me and was causing him to feel increasingly ambivalent about therapy, he would deprecate me and my efforts to be helpful.

One afternoon he came to his appointment and announced that he had moved in with Robert. He loved Robert, he said, and wanted to spend as much time as possible with him. To do so he planned to spend less time working and had quit a job that had been very gratifying.

John was shocked when his wife initiated divorce proceedings and by the amount of the financial settlement she was demanding. His attorney suggested he keep his relationship with Robert secret since, if it became known, she might want to use it to restrict visitation rights with his children. Soon thereafter he, Robert, and John's nine-year-old child went on an afternoon excursion to the Metropolitan Museum. When I questioned the appropriateness of his doing so, he became furious, again claiming that I was keeping him from "becoming gay."

The next day he canceled his appointment, leaving the message that he was looking for another therapist. I called him to try to get him to discuss his decision. He claimed that attorney's fees and the anticipated financial settlement with his wife had made therapy too expensive. "Furthermore," he said, "this therapy is taking too much time away from Robert." I asked him to call me whenever he might wish to do so. About two weeks later, he found another therapist, a social worker, whose office was closer to his own than mine had been. "The commute would not be so time-consuming and difficult," he told me. My impression was that his increased need for me since the separation from his wife had frightened and enraged him.

About eight months later his gay friend called to tell me that John had committed suicide and that his body had been found in a motel room in another state. He had seen two more therapists but had found none to be satisfactory. The relationship with Robert had deteriorated. John had wanted to return home; his wife did not want him to. He left no note of explanation.

John had a chronic, atypical depression. Whenever he felt

dependent on anyone for nurturance and support, he experienced unconscious rage at the prospect of being abandoned and vindictively left before being left. His mother's emotional absence when he was an infant and, possibly, her abrupt physical as well as emotional withdrawal when a six-years-younger sibling was born, made him vulnerable to the abandonment of others and to the fury he experienced whenever he felt dependent. His father, whom he felt to be perfectionistic, demanding, and preoccupied with his own professional advancement, could not compensate for John's earliest emotional neglect from his mother.

Although he had sought help to be more out as a gay man, he experienced his homosexuality as his most profound imperfection; he was certain that he would not be loved unless he was perfect. His homosexuality was the expression of desire for a sexual and loving relationship with another man, but through his sexual behavior he also expressed rage toward his wife, children, mother, and father, which led to guilt, hopelessness, and, ultimately, suicide.

For any middle-aged homosexual man to separate and divorce without suffering more than realistic pain from this loss, it is necessary that he view his sexual orientation positively. And, if this is to occur, he must have a healthy, realistically positive self-regard. If self-esteem has been severely damaged from childhood injury or neglect, as it had been for John, then homosexual feelings and impulses will also be consciously or unconsciously negatively valued, and sexuality that is experienced as part of a bad, sick, or sinful self will likely be used to express hurt and rage.[7]

John was the only married homosexual man I have worked with who did kill himself, but several of the middle-aged men who have consulted me had thought of suicide. My sample, of course, is not random, since any married homosexual man who consults a therapist feels in conflict about his situation and may, therefore, be clinically depressed.

In her survey of homosexual and bisexual men who were or had been married, Catherine Whitney quoted the following letter, which was written by the former wife of a homosexual man:

> We had been married eight years when I found out my husband was having an affair with a man. He left me to live with his new lover, but their relationship only lasted a few months, and he begged me to take him back. He promised me that he would give up being gay, that it was only a passing phase. But after two years, I found out he had had another affair and I asked him to leave. He begged me to give him one more chance and promised to get therapy for his problem. But I couldn't handle it anymore, and I told him no. Several weeks later he checked into a hotel and took an overdose of drugs.[8]

Whitney also quotes a psychologist who had taped a man who had called in to his radio show threatening to kill himself:

> His voice was all choked up. He said he was calling from his car phone, and he was parked near a bridge. He said he'd been driving there with the intention of committing suicide, but he heard me on the air and stopped the car and called. . . . He was fifty-two years old, married for twenty-six years, with two adult children. He felt as though he had been living a lie for years . . . but he believed it was too late for him—he had missed his chance. "Can you imagine me walking into a gay bar?" he asked. "I wouldn't know what to do at this point. For me to act on my leanings now would ruin my life and my family's life."[9]

It is not useful for the clinician to view John's suicide as being simply the result of his depression. I do believe that it is helpful to recognize that any middle-aged homosexual man in a long heterosexual marriage poses a serious suicide risk; he is likely to believe that there is no other solution to the dilemma caused by conflict between his fear of loss of love and security and the inherent, compelling need to express his sexuality in a loving relationship with another man.

Calvin

Calvin was successful in making the difficult transition from a heterosexual marriage to a gratifying relationship with a man. I will try to document some of the reasons he was able to do so.

He was forty years old, had been married for eighteen years, and had two teenage children when he sought help. He loved his wife and children but felt passionless, unhappy, unfulfilled, and inauthentic. He was exhausted by a constant need to maintain the disguise of heterosexuality with his family and colleagues. He longed for a loving relationship with another man.

Calvin had always considered himself to be homosexual. For as long as he could remember, his fantasies had been predominantly homoerotic. He had been in one relationship for nearly two years when he was about eighteen. It was stormy but passionate and he had felt very much in love. He stopped seeing his lover because of the disapproval of his parents, particularly his father, who insisted that he seek therapy because of his homosexuality.

He entered treatment and, with the explicit urging of his therapist, began to pursue heterosexual relationships. Calvin found sex with women pleasurable, although not as satisfying as his homosexual encounters. He did not feel the same connection to women that he had experienced with men. Nevertheless, he did marry while he was in treatment and gave up homosexual sex, maintaining a "pretty good" sexual relationship with his wife for the first two or three years of marriage. He started therapy again when he was about thirty because of his decreasing sexual desire for his wife.

When he sought consultation Calvin had just stopped this second treatment. With bitterness he informed me that both of his previous therapists had viewed his homosexuality as a phobic response to female genitals. He was confused, depressed, fearful, and, at times, quite suicidal because he felt hopelessly divided between commitment to his family and a strong desire for a loving, passionate attachment to another man.

Most helpful to Calvin at the beginning of his therapy was my conveying understanding of his conflict. But I also implicitly affirmed his need to pursue his homosexual desire by accepting his homosexuality as an inherent and integral part of his nature and not as a defense against inhibited heterosexuality. Like the previous patients, he knew I was gay and that I had also been married, which he had heard prior to starting therapy.

Over the ensuing months Calvin began to experiment safely with a variety of sexual partners; within one year he was also meeting gay men for nonsexual friendships. He was excited by rediscovering his passion and was comfortable and surprisingly unconflicted about his homosexuality. The clinical depression gradually began to lift.

Within the first year of therapy he was confronted by his wife about his lack of sexual interest and his increasingly frequent late nights away from home. He told her then about his longstanding homosexual interest and his renewed sexual encounters and passion. Within a few months they had agreed to a trial separation.

Calvin's mother had been alcoholic; his father was emotionally detached and during much of Calvin's later childhood was in Europe on assignment for the government. Calvin had felt lonely and unloved as a child and now recognized that he had spent much of his life trying to please his parents by his choice of profession as well as by attempting to give up his homosexuality, marrying, and having children. He also recognized that he had married to comply with the conviction of his previous therapists that he would be happier and healthier being heterosexual.

Both of his therapists had helped Calvin comprehend and deal with his rage over the deprivations of his childhood. Because his self-esteem had been less impaired than John's, he was gradually able to have reasonably conflict-free and pleasurable sexual contacts. Also helping to consolidate his positive feeling about himself as a gay man were the warm and supportive friendships with other gay men that he was forming, his sexual experiences within the context of affectionate relationships, and coming out to his colleagues.

About two years after separating from his wife, Calvin had to stop therapy. However, I did have the opportunity to follow his progress since he saw me from time to time during the following year and then kept in telephone contact.

Shortly after stopping treatment, he met a young man with whom he fell in love, and after a few months they decided to live together. His partner provided him with the passion and emotional intensity that he had never before experienced and had always desired. His love and continuous support helped Calvin deal with the loneliness that he often felt because of the loss of his family and friends and leaving treatment.

John and Calvin came to treatment with similar complaints and history. Both had been dissatisfied with the lack of love and passion in their lives as married men. Both had sustained significant self-esteem damage from emotional neglect in childhood. Both had been in psychoanalytically oriented treatment in which heterosexual sex and marriage were encouraged as solutions to their homosexuality by therapists who viewed homosexuality as a symptom of inhibited heterosexuality. Each analyst had unwittingly exploited his patient's transference need to be loved by his father to get him to pursue heterosexual relationships and eventual marriage.

Taking note of their dissimilarity, however, is particularly instructive in understanding the needs and appropriate therapy for homosexual men in unsatisfying marriages. John was the more eager to be open about his sexuality at the onset of his therapy and to dissolve his long marriage in order to do so. Unlike Calvin, he denied that he was angered by the emotional neglect he had sustained in childhood and was inclined, therefore, to express this anger in self-injurious ways. Impulsively leaving his wife and children in order to make himself feel less depressed eventually led to being rejected by her, which reinforced his conviction that he was unlovable and contributed to his sense of hopelessness and eventual suicide.

Although his two previous analysts had not enabled Calvin to acknowledge his homosexuality and thereby to begin to become gay, they did greatly enhance his capacity to tolerate and express anger. Unlike John, Calvin felt safe and trusting enough to make use of the relationship with me to reexperience and then work through rageful feelings toward his rejecting and often absent father. The reworking of this old relationship in the transference enabled him to avoid repeating the experience of rejection in his new relationships. Understanding the childhood origins of his anger, he was able to experience affection for and from me, which facilitated his capacity to form friendships that were warm and supportive outside of therapy, and, eventually and most important, to fall in love. He had established a strong and positive gay identity as part of his increasingly positive self-regard.

Bisexuals in Marriage

Men whose sexual fantasies are divided about equally between the same and the opposite sex usually are able to experience sexual pleasure with both men and women. They often have had the experience of being attracted to both, but my clinical experience and personal observation have suggested that they are only inclined to experience love for and from women. For this reason and for purposes of social acceptance, most bisexual men in our society choose conventional marriages.

Unlike homosexual men, bisexuals are generally satisfied in their heterosexual marriages because of the emotional and sexual gratification they are able to obtain. For a bisexual man to live a gratifying, exclusively heterosexual life, however, he also has to be comfortable with his homosexual fantasies and impulses and have the capacity to use these fantasies in the service of his heterosexual activity. If he cannot accept the homosexual component of his sexual orientation, then, like a married homosexual man, he will usually be dissatisfied in his marriage. Some who are comfortable with the homosexual aspect of their bisexuality may need homosexual experiences to maintain the stability of their marriage.

True bisexuality in men is probably rare.[10] However, since bisexual men accommodate to a marriage with relatively less conflict and stress than homosexual men, and, in all likelihood, most do not seek help, it is difficult to know just how prevalent bisexuality is. Most of the men I have seen who label themselves bisexual do so simply because they are in conflict about being homosexual. I have worked with only three men over the past fifteen years whom I considered to be truly bisexual. One of these bisexual men had a long-lasting relationship with a woman with whom he had a child, although they never married.[11] Another remained married while having numerous homosexual liaisons. The third was Claude.

Claude was thirty years old and had been married for five years when he first saw me because he was unhappy in his marriage. He had a history of bisexual activity from about age sixteen, when he had both a boyfriend and a girlfriend. He was excited by women and proud of being able to give them multiple orgasms by maintaining his erection for prolonged periods.

Except for a two-year relationship as an adolescent, Claude's sexual activity with men tended to be more random and anonymous than with women. He usually had sex in the rest room of his college library; occasionally he would develop a crush on someone and see him more than once. Although he seemed to be able to relate to women more easily than to men and to fall in love with women and not with men, he was equally attracted to both.

Claude was the older of two children. His mother apparently had difficulty caring for him as an infant because of depression caused by the death of her favorite sibling. She had one or two miscarriages before his sister was born. His father, warm but preoccupied and somewhat distant, could not provide him with much-needed love and support.

Claude felt jealous of his sister. He was told he should not be angry with her and never to hit her, which made him feel guilty and obliged to constrain his rage over the attention she demanded. At the age of seven or eight he began to dress in his mother's clothes; he had decided that if he couldn't be angry with his sister, then he'd become like her. His earliest sexual partners in high school were, in fact, his sister's girlfriends and one of her boyfriends. As an adult he continued to occasionally cross-dress in order to pick men up.

I saw Claude three times weekly in analytically oriented therapy for about two years and then twice weekly and once a week for several more years. When I first started to work with him, his first marriage was deteriorating because of his wife's frequent absences and her lack of attention and appreciation. He divorced her during his second year of therapy. Soon thereafter he met a woman with whom he fell in love.

His cross-dressing abated over time as Claude understood that he was jealous of both parents' attention to his sister and that he had been trying to look like her. His homosexual fantasies and impulses, however, did not abate; when he felt neglected by his wife, he would go on the Internet to find sex.

He is devoted to his second wife. She knows of his bisexuality and is not threatened by his occasional need to have sex with men. The success of his marriage will depend upon his continuing to find sexual and emotional gratification in his marriage, on his ability to satisfy his wife's needs, and on her continuing ability to understand his need to express his homosexual feelings. It will also depend on Claude's capacity to acknowledge his anger when he feels slighted and jealous and to express his bisexuality in ways that do not threaten or demean his wife.

The Therapeutic Task

Any therapist of a heterosexually married homosexual man in mid-adulthood must be understanding of the loving ties his patient usually has to his spouse and children and the pain and difficulty he may have in leaving his marriage. Lack of empathy for this aspect of his dilemma will cause the patient to feel just as misunderstood and unsupported as would his therapist's inability to empathize with the need to express his sexuality in a loving attachment to another man. Nor should the clinician anticipate that the strength of homosexual desire alone will be enough to mitigate significantly the pain of loss that occurs when these marriages deteriorate. He has to clarify and then help his patient make a realistic and reasonable assessment of the importance, on the one hand, of the gratification obtained from social respectability and a longstanding relationship with spouse and children and, on the other hand, of the desire to feel more authentic by expressing his inherent sexuality and establishing a personal and social identity as a gay man.

For the self-esteem enhancement necessary for the resolution of this conflict, the patient must first understand the nature of those narcissistic injuries that consciously or unconsciously motivated him to marry in order to gain a sense of social approbation and, thereby, a feeling of self-worth. He should then, through understanding and the reworking in the transference of his parental relationships, become less self-hating and less dependent on the approval of others. As he grows genuinely more affirming of himself, he will become more accepting of his homosexuality. Those who wish or need to remain married, like the first patient, Peter, are then enabled to feel less isolated because they have greater access to and are more accepting of their sexual desire, although they may choose not to express it.

The understanding and repair of self-esteem injury is only the first step, albeit a crucial one, for those who desire to make the mid-life transition from marriage to what they perceive as a more passionate and authentic life. Those who are able to do so successfully have also been helped by a therapist knowledgeable about the developmental steps necessary for establishing a healthy identity as a gay man: to have passionate sexual experiences; to come out when possible; to form friendships with other gay men; and to sustain sexual, intimate, and mutually loving relationships. These developmental steps are essential not only to enhance the quality of life but to equip them to deal better with the losses, slights, indignities, and injuries that often accompany being openly gay in our society.

Heterosexual marriages may work for some, but over time they usually contribute to a homosexual man's feeling isolated, lonely, inauthentic, and frustrated, as the case histories have illustrated. In general, I believe that any homosexual man will live a healthier, more gratifying life if he is able to express his sexual orientation in an intimate sexual relationship with another man in which he feels loved and loving.

Whether it is a gay man who discovers his somnolent homosexual passion and longing for the love of another man or a heterosexual who rediscovers heterosexual desire after years of decreasing passion, the search for renewed passion in middle age is not uncommon. The awareness of the physical signs of aging, altered relationships with parents or children, the death of parents, relatives, or friends, and the perception of diminished sexual and physical prowess all remind us of the limitations of time and evoke anxiety about death and dying.[12] Both homosexual and heterosexual men describe their resurgent sexuality in mid-life as life-giving.

Perhaps there is a phylogenetic, biologically determined need for rebirth in middle age, which may partly explain why many men and women seek a new life path at that time. For, "life after forty—the eras of middle adulthood and beyond—has been a significant part of man's collective experience for but a moment in our history."[13]

5 Developing a Positive Gay Identity with HIV or AIDS

The thirst for eternity is what is called love among men and whoever loves another wishes to eternalize himself in him.

—MIGUEL DE UNAMUNO

Trauma is defined as a shocking or frightening event that causes symptoms because the event exceeds one's capacity to cope with the evoked anxiety.[1] The term "traumatic effect" is usually used to refer to those symptoms produced by such an event or to the inhibiting or retarding effect of the trauma on some aspect of development.

Being informed that one is HIV positive or has AIDS does not usually produce the traumatic effect one might anticipate—severe clinical depression.[2] However, anyone who is told that he is infected with a potentially fatal virus and anyone whose illness subsequently progresses to AIDS will likely develop some degree of anxiety or depression for periods of time because of the overwhelming task of coping with the fear of deteriorating health, fear of the illness's effect on relationships and the capacity to work, and fear of death.[3]

As the psychologist Gordon Allport wrote,

> It sometimes happens that the very center of organization of a personality shifts suddenly and apparently without warning. Some impetus, coming perhaps from a bereavement, an illness, or a religious conversion, even from a teacher or a book, may lead to a reorientation . . . a traumatic recentering. What once seemed to him cold, "out there," "not mine," may change places and become hot and vital, "in here," "mine."[4]

Being told that one is HIV positive, acknowledging that one is HIV positive, or knowing one has AIDS often causes just such a traumatic recentering of the personality. The trauma may provide the impetus for some gay men to come out. Most important, it has enabled some to be able to fall in love and to establish and maintain a loving relationship for the first time.

Between 1985 and 1995 I was consulted by about twenty homosexual men infected with HIV and treated nine of them in insight-oriented therapy. Two had sessions four times a week in psychoanalysis; the others came either once or twice weekly. One man died after only seven months; the others worked with me for at least two years. Two of my nine patients sought help before they were able to acknowledge to themselves that they were infected, although in therapy their behavior and recollection suggested they had the preconscious perception that they were. One man came for treatment after having been tested and told he was HIV positive; the others sought help after having signs or symptoms of AIDS. They ranged in age from twenty-five to forty years.

Arnold

Arnold was the oldest of four siblings raised in a Catholic home. Both of his parents, and particularly his mother, he believed, were more concerned about his being well behaved than about his needs or feelings. He thought they preferred his two older sisters, who were less rebellious, less sexual.

Arnold's earliest sexual experiences were when he was five with a neighbor's child who was seven or eight. Arnold's mother discovered these dalliances, chastised him, and sent him to talk to the parish priest. As an adolescent he experimented surreptitiously with both boys and girls, but his most persistent experience was as a high school junior with his math teacher, with whom he regularly masturbated. He felt used by this older man but was also attracted to him and had considerable affection for him.

During college Arnold had occasional sex with two of his classmates, always feeling depressed and guilty afterward. In medical school he remained uncomfortable about being homosexual, too uncomfortable to meet other gay men in social situations; so he often went to the baths, where he could have sexual encounters anonymously. He would go not only when he was horny or lonely but when he needed to be comforted by attention and soothed by sex after he had felt hurt from some personal or social slight. Inevitably he became furious at his sexual partners for admiring and then using his body or for being concerned about their pleasure and oblivious of his needs for affection. Finishing, he felt dirty, sinful, disgusted, guilty, and depressed.

Arnold moved to New York in 1982 to begin his residency training, starting his analysis with me in May 1985, when he was twenty-nine. He had briefly seen another therapist, who, he believed, had been focused more on helping him to understand why he was homosexual than on the problems he was experiencing in a new relationship and in his residency program, which he considered homophobic.

About two weeks after starting analysis, Arnold came out to two friends, one gay and one straight. Then he told his older sister he was homosexual. He claimed it was the comfort he found in talking to me that had enabled him to come out. I was perplexed by how soon after beginning treatment this was occurring and did not then understand that the motive for telling people about his sexual orientation was a preconscious fear that he was already infected with HIV.

He related that his sister had been afraid that he might have AIDS and was reluctant to let him hold his niece. He was outraged at her rejecting behavior, believing that she was expressing prejudice about his homosexuality, a conviction I thought at the time to be correct. It was only a few weeks later that I understood he had probably either conveyed to her some concern that he was already infected or she had noticed some change in his physical appearance.

Arnold had not told me that for several months he had been feeling more fatigued than usual. He was not withholding this information; he appeared simply not to have noticed it. Only after being in analysis for about three months did he mention, in an offhand manner, that he had been having chills and night sweats for a couple of weeks. He thought these symptoms had been caused by his anxiety from frightening dreams. It was then, for the first time, that he wondered whether he might have AIDS, and he became terrified.

I was also frightened. I silently worried that he might have mentioned these symptoms before and, out of my need to deny that he was sick, I had not heard him. I even briefly wondered whether his concern about AIDS could be a manifestation of his unresolved guilt about being homosexual. These musings occurred during the minute or so I had needed before being able to acknowledge that this handsome, intelligent young man, who was just beginning his career and his first relationship, was going to die.

I also then understood that, in telling me of his sister's response to his coming out, he had been attempting to let me know that he feared he was infected and that it was a perception of being HIV positive, rather than his psychoanalysis, that had allowed him, after so many years of silence, to begin to come out.

Arnold consulted an AIDS specialist, who found precariously few T cells and diagnosed "pre-AIDS."* He wept in telling me how much care he would need as he became sicker and how frightened he was that his lover and his friends would not want to take care of him. He was convinced that I would not have wanted to treat him had I known he was sick. He was frightened of his parents' rejection and concerned about damage to his career when teachers and colleagues found out. He regretted that he might not live to benefit from his understanding of himself, from his recent acceptance of his homosexuality, or from the happiness he was just beginning to experience in a relationship that "makes me feel alive."

When he returned to analysis in September after my three-week vacation, I noticed that Arnold had lost considerable weight; he appeared haggard and exhausted. He had been sleeping fitfully and was relieved to be back seeing me, since he believed that doing so would enhance his sense of emotional well-being, which, in turn, might help his flagging immune system. In one hour, shortly after he returned, he spoke of this hopefulness:

*At that time counting the number of T cells was used to track the functioning of the immune system and, thereby, susceptibility to opportunistic infections and AIDS.

I think there's a good chance that everything will be okay, even though another part of me feels that I could get sick and die. It scares me that I know there might be mechanisms that make me want to get sick and stay sick. I'm glad I am in analysis. . . . Maybe I'll learn here not to make myself so miserable. I really believe this is one of those illnesses where psychological factors go into it. It's so variable what happens. . . . One of my friends has lymphadenopathy. He's had it for two years and nothing else. I'll have to live with this uncertainty for years.

Arnold's health, however, continued to deteriorate, but although his fevers were becoming more debilitating, he would not accept the protocol for the experimental immune enhancer that his physician wanted him to try. He feared the medication would damage his health even more rapidly, leaving him too sick to be cared for at home and needing to be hospitalized. He feared being hospitalized at his training site, since his teachers and supervisors would then know he was homosexual. He was relieved that his physician had privileges at another teaching hospital, and arranged to be cared for there should the need ever arise.

In early November he missed an appointment because of the "flu." While I was away for the weekend, his lover left a message that he had been hospitalized.

Returning home, I found another message: he had died. He had developed acute respiratory symptoms from pneumocystis pneumonia. His physician had wanted to do a tracheotomy and place him on a respirator to assist his labored breathing, but Arnold had refused him permission to do so. He died a few hours later.

In the hospital Arnold had confided to his lover that he was afraid he would have recurrent, debilitating infections and illnesses: he did not want to suffer, he did not want to be a burden to others, he did not want to deal with the stigma connected with AIDS and being gay.

Arnold used his therapy to make significant changes in his life in a short time. He came into treatment ambivalently acknowledging his homosexuality but was out to only a very few people and to no one in his family. Coming out to two colleagues helped him feel more positively about being gay. Although the experience of coming out to his sister was hurtful and aggravating, he was emboldened by having been able to do so.

Arnold had met his lover, Tom, less than one year before beginning treatment with me, and his main goal in starting analysis had been to deal with the problems he was having in his relationship and with the difficulty feeling that Tom loved him. He knew that anxiety about intimacy had previously kept him from forming relationships. He was concerned that his anxiety would continue to interfere with his capacity to love in this relationship.

In a few months after beginning treatment, a surprisingly short time, he understood enough about the association of this anxiety with fear of his mother's criticism and with rage at her and his father because of their seeming indifference toward him, that the relationship with Tom began to improve significantly.

There is often a honeymoon at the start of any therapy or analysis when patients who are favorably disposed to their therapist accept interpretations without much resistance or defensiveness. They want to please the therapist and to be liked. But Arnold's lack of resistance extended beyond the early weeks of our work; it could not be sufficiently explained by his comfort with me, or his wish to be liked, or even his characteristic tendency to passivity and compliance. In retrospect, his capacity to do psychotherapeutic work and make changes in his life was enhanced or even caused by preconscious knowledge that he was HIV positive, which made him more focused, less resistant, and better able to integrate my comments and observations than someone who is HIV negative. My recognition that our work together would be time-limited undoubtedly also made me more focused and engaged.[5]

As important as they were, Arnold's ultimately successful attempts to understand longstanding fears of intimacy and to alter his negative feelings about his homosexuality and his perception of himself as a gay man were used to deny that he was HIV positive, that he was becoming symptomatic, and that he might die. His focus in therapy on conflicts about intimacy and the relationship with his parents paradoxically strengthened his denial by helping him believe that he would live not only a long life but a more fulfilling one as well. He seemed to have the irrational hope at the beginning of treatment, shared by many confronting fatal illness, that he was neurotic rather than physically ill, and could be cured. Perhaps he also had the magical wish that if he started analysis, a therapy that takes a long time, he would live a long life.

I had seen this man for only seven months when he died. He was my second patient to develop AIDS and the first to die. I felt utterly helpless. Although I have grieved over the death of every patient, none has distressed me as much as Arnold's, for I found him to be a particularly likable man. He had a self-effacing and self-deprecating manner that touched me but that also was symptomatic of his masochistic character. Although society's prejudice had contributed to his self-hatred for being homosexual, and society's failure to sanction same-sex love had made it more comfortable for him to seek out anonymous sexual partners than relationships, his need to limit gratification and pleasure had also kept him from loving and feeling loved.

We did not have enough time to understand much about the injury to his self-esteem that caused these masochistic character traits; however, my impression was that, feeling rejected by both parents, constantly rebuked by his critical mother and overlooked by his uninvolved father, he became excessively self-critical and, at times, even self-destructive as a way of controlling his anger and fear of being disappointed by them and others. Now that he was sick, nothing worse could happen, and he no longer had to seek out pain or limit his pleasure. He was then able to find contentment and gratification in the loving relationship that he had never permitted himself to experience before.[6]

David

David came to see me in 1980 because he was depressed and felt isolated and believed that he would never be able to have an intimate relationship. He told me that he had always been depressed. His mother had never expressed warmth or affection; she had loved him, he said, simply because he was talented and smart. His father was much warmer than she but preferred his younger brother, who was more masculine, athletic, and companionable. David was filled with rage, which, like Arnold's, was repressed and directed against himself. As a consequence, he also placed himself in dangerous situations, especially in seeking sex.

From the time he began to have sex as a third-year college student, he preferred hustlers. Some would emotionally abuse him. On one or two occasions in medical school his apartment was robbed and he was physically threatened; once his car was stolen. In spite of his financial generosity, these exploitive young men would inevitably leave him, infuriated by David's manipulativeness or made increasingly uncomfortable by their dependence on him. These relationships appeared to recapture the experience of both his mother's abusiveness and his father's unattainable love.

David hated being homosexual. He thought of himself as sick and repeatedly reminded me that he was "perverse." He asked me to help him to have heterosexual sex so that he could give his parents the grandchildren they longed for. He wanted to be heterosexual so that his father would love him as much as he loved his heterosexual, outgoing younger brother.

David also hated his body. He thought that his hips, thighs, and buttocks were more like a woman's than a man's. His persistent desire to be dominated and anally penetrated also made him feel feminine and revolted him, reminding him of the ways in which he was like his mother. He avoided associating with other gay men who were effeminate, because he believed they called attention to his own femininity.

I had been treating David for about one year when, in June 1981, the Center for Disease Control reported that five previously healthy gay men had developed pneumocystis pneumonia. In July they reported that Kaposi's sarcoma had been found in twenty-six gay men during the previous thirty months. Within a year, the CDC was suggesting that this illness was sexually transmitted.[7]

I informed David explicitly of the potential dangers of his indiscriminate sexual behavior, telling him what little I knew about the nature of what was then being called GRID (Gay-Related Immune Deficiency), the possible ways it could be transmitted, and the steps he might take to keep from acquiring it. David was in his last year of medical school, but he disavowed having any knowledge of the disease, questioned whether it even existed, and wondered whether my concern was an expression of my homophobia.

He continued to question the validity of my information and my motives for speaking with him about it. Aside from wondering whether I was homophobic, he believed I was jealous of his sexual prowess. He exhorted me to be more analytic and objective and less concerned about his health. My concern, evoking a desire to be taken care of, frightened and infuriated him—he experienced me as being like his mother and had little recognition of how his needs were separate from mine. He was also afraid that when he felt close to me his rage would either destroy me or drive me away, and, we learned later, any affectionate feelings evoked erotic thoughts that frightened him.

David felt contempt for me because he believed I was gay, but, like many other young psychiatrists and psychologists in training at that time, he never asked me about my sexual orientation, rationalizing away his curiosity as being inappropriate. And I, then still married, was relieved not to be asked. My complicity at the beginning of his analysis with David's reluctance to make personal inquiries about my homosexuality deprived us of an early opportunity to understand his anxiety about having sexual feelings for me and to deepen our understanding of his homophobia.

In the fall of 1985 David told me that he was having diarrhea and night sweats and that he had noticed swollen lymph nodes. He thought he had the flu, treated himself with Tylenol, and refused to see a physician.

Arnold had died a few weeks after David first mentioned his symptoms; several other patients had, by then, consulted me because of their anxiety about either having AIDS or contracting it. I had one friend and several acquaintances who were sick, and, of course, I also felt it was possible that I could be infected. My attempt to give David advice was the only way I had of trying to exert control over the effect this disease was having on my own life.

I suggested he see one of the growing number of physicians who were working with AIDS patients. He refused, frustrating and irritating me, reactions he would try to elicit to make himself feel I noticed and cared about him and was not neglecting him. My irritation also enabled him to maintain a sense of some boundary between us, which he had been unable to experience with his mother.

By now, five years into his therapy, David was more accepting of his homosexuality than he had been at the beginning of treatment. He understood that he had been repulsed by it because he experienced being homosexual and the desire to be close to his father as being like his mother. He also now understood more about the ways he had internalized society's hatred of homosexuals. The progress he made in dealing with his own homophobia helped him, as it had Arnold, to express his sexuality in less self-destructive and more gratifying ways. And his new understanding and recent good feeling helped him to feel hopeful about his future.

Three months after first telling me of his night sweats and swollen lymph nodes, David mentioned that he had met a graduate student at a bar near his apartment. They saw each other often during the following weeks and soon David fell in love. They were affectionate and caring of one another, and their relationship grew with surprising rapidity. After a couple of months they entered into a joint business venture. The following year, Andrew moved into David's apartment. They remained together throughout David's illness and until his death. From the time they met, David never again had sex with a hustler, nor did he have much inclination to do so.

About six months after meeting Andrew, David finally consulted a physician. On the second visit he was told that his T cells were very low. The next day he told me how frightened he was and that he was worried about how long he had to live. He spoke about Andrew: "He never looked so beautiful as he did yesterday. I feel more alive with him than I ever felt before. There aren't words to describe what he means to me. He is a constant source of support. I hope I live long enough to enjoy him."

He said that the relationship made him feel stable and centered, that he no longer yearned for physical comfort from strangers. He recognized how much more receptive he was to being loved than ever before.

Jay

Jay further illustrates how having AIDS can enable someone to love.

He was thirty-five when he sought help after his first bout of pneumocystis pneumonia. Two months before becoming ill, Jay had noticed enlarged lymph nodes and a periodic low-grade fever but had paid little attention to these signs of infection. Now, since his hospitalization, he was frightened and depressed and began to experience obsessional thoughts.

He had met his lover after having become infected, and, as with David and Arnold, it was his first significant relationship. Jay, however, was more comfortable with his homosexuality than they had been. He had been out to his siblings and his parents for about ten years; Arnold had not come out to his sisters and David to his family until the year each had developed symptoms.

Jay told me that by the age of seven or eight he knew he was attracted to other boys, and with the onset of puberty he had become aware of his desire to be anally penetrated. He desired older men who were stronger than he and could dominate him. He worked out daily, not only to look attractive to other men but to tone his muscles so that he would feel less feminine.

During two years of therapy, Jay spoke about early childhood experiences that he had found disturbing. He had been particularly distressed by his relationship with his father, who he felt competed with him and tried to diminish and humiliate him at every opportunity. Jay recognized that this humiliation had at times been sexually stimulating and that being dominated in sex now evoked these same excited feelings.

Like Arnold and David, he was repulsed by anal-receptive sexual fantasies and the feminine feelings they awakened. It became, in fact, difficult for him, and for me as well, to understand how much his feeling contaminated stemmed from having AIDS and how much was due to his repugnance toward a longstanding desire for anal sex that made him "feminine."

Jay had been in casual relationships most of his adult life. Because prospective lovers made him feel as his father had—abused, excited, humiliated, and furious—he drove them away. He was much more comfortable in one-night stands or relationships of a few weeks that did not evoke these complex feelings.

Nine months before he noted his swollen lymph nodes, Jay met his lover. They were immediately attracted to each other and found that they had many interests in common. After a short courtship, Jay, who had always lived alone, decided they should share an apartment. It was the first time he had ever fallen in love. Anxiety and anger no longer inhibited his capacity for a relationship. He now felt capable of loving as well as being loved.

After talking to me for many hours about the way he feared AIDS would affect his life and his future and experiencing some diminution of anxiety, he spent most of his time with me, until he became very sick, talking about his relationship and the concern he had about getting close to Joshua. He knew it had been difficult for him to be close to other men for any length of time, and he was concerned that this familiar anxiety might also cause him to push Joshua away. Jay was already experiencing Joshua's requests for affection and sex as demands that made him want to withdraw, and the angry disputations that usually followed his withdrawal made him feel unlovable and depressed.

Like both David and Arnold, Jay confronted his psychological conflicts with surprising ease and rapidity, integrating insights without as much resistance as most HIV-negative patients. In the slightly less than three years we worked together, he gained understanding about how being close to and dependent on Joshua evoked a fear of humiliation and, at the same time, erotic feelings for his father. He was able to maintain a warm and loving relationship with Joshua until his death.

About six months before his death, one week after being told he had an inoperable tumor, Jay had the following dream: "I am going with Joshua into the Lincoln Tunnel. It begins to leak and I get panicked. He leads me to the other side." His associations had mainly to do with fear of loss of control of his bladder and bowels, which terrified him, for he was usually confident of his capacity to control himself as well as other people. But other associations followed: "I am not lonely now that Joshua is around. I don't need sex anymore to make me feel in touch. Just being close to him makes me feel warm. I want to be alive with him."

David, even after being told that his T-cell ratio was dangerously low, had said his lover made him "feel more alive than I have ever felt before." Arnold, afraid that he would not live to benefit from a new understanding of himself, had also exclaimed that his relationship made him feel alive.

How can we understand that each of these patients had met his lover after he was infected and within two years of death, and that for each it was his first sustained, mutually loving relationship? One reason, although not the only explanation, is that each had previously limited the pleasure and gratification in his life to master and control the pain anticipated from future disappointments. Because they were infected, each of these men was now able to permit himself the gratification of a long-sought but heretofore elusive love.

No patient more clearly illustrates how HIV may free one to seek a more gratifying life than Hugh. He was thirty-nine when I started to treat him in 1993. Because of falling T cells, he was planning his retirement from a successful academic career. He had no symptoms but wanted the freedom to travel while his health was still good.

Hugh had begun to shoplift in high school, attempting to compensate for feeling deprived by his mother's stinginess, strictness, and relentless ambition for him. Over the following years this shoplifting became habitual and more and more obvious; he was caught on several occasions. Twice he had to hire an attorney, who averted his being charged and expelled from school.

In 1983, during his second year of graduate school, he had two bouts of "flu." He now believes that even at the time he knew he was infected with HIV, although he did not get tested until several years later. After these illnesses, he had no further impulse to shoplift. He lost his sense of rage over his mother's harshness and his father's detachment. He seemed to feel no further need to inflict punishment on himself. By the time I started to treat him, Hugh was in his first relationship, then in its fifth year. He had met his lover one year after getting tested.

The masochistic inclinations and impulses of some homosexual men usually derive from damage to their self-esteem
caused by early paternal disinterest or rejection, later peer rejection, and society's hatred. They seek pain and severely limit
pleasure and gratification in an effort to control rage over the
anticipated rejections and disappointments of the future.

There is greater vulnerability to such rejection, as we have
seen with David, Arnold, and Hugh, when there has been an
exploitive, binding, or impoverished relationship with the
mother. Then the father is looked to even earlier and with
greater fervor for the soothing, comfort, and loving attachment
the mother cannot provide. But any homosexual man, drawn
as he is to his father, will limit acceptance of love in future relationships, sometimes even seeking pain in them, if he has felt
rejected by his father. Mother's rejection makes the father's
rebuff, distance, or indifference even more painful, but paternal rejection is the usual although not a sufficient explanation
for a gay man's self-esteem injury and for the masochistic inclinations that often follow.

The gratification of masochistic impulses by the prospect of
death does not alone explain why gay men with HIV are able
to permit themselves to fall in love and maintain a relationship,
often for the first time in their lives. Infected men and women
from all risk groups appear to find ways to build confidence in
their future, and falling in love is one important way of doing
so.[8] Hopefulness serves to ward off the overwhelming anxiety,
depression, and suicidal impulses that one might reasonably
expect to be present, but that are surprisingly absent, in most
patients with AIDS.[9]

Gay men in general have a greater capacity to cope with
stress than heterosexual men, I believe, because throughout
their lives they have had to deal with the stress of feeling alienated from mainstream heterosexual society and have had to

find ways to contend with hatred and rejection. Overcoming longstanding anxiety or fear of intimate relationships, because of an anticipated need to be cared for in the future, is also adaptive to the stresses and demands imposed by their illness.

Accompanying the normal aging process is an increased awareness of the limited time one has to reach vocational goals and to satisfy or achieve congruity between one's internal needs and external social demands and expectations. What one must do to achieve happiness and a sense of tranquility must be done now if it is to be done at all. Most gay men with HIV or AIDS have the time perspective of those who are in late middle age or of the elderly. Because of their confrontation with mortality, they have had a clearer recognition than before their illness of those needs and desires that had previously seemed impossible to achieve or had evoked so much anxiety that they were repressed and unknowable.[10]

HIV may also make it possible to confront and overcome the anxiety of intimacy by occasioning a reordering of priorities. As Yallom and Greaves wrote: "As one's focus turns from the trivial diversions of life, a fuller appreciation of the elemental factors in existence may emerge."[11]

Being able to fall in love or to be in a loving relationship with HIV and AIDS, however, is due to more than the gratification of masochistic needs, more than the enhanced capacity to adapt to stress, more than denial, and even more than courage in the face of death. Being loved and loving cause those infected to hope that they will not die so that they might live forever in their state of happiness and contentment. For each of us longs not to die. As it has always been and always will be, loving and feeling loved are ways humans have of satisfying their quest for eternity and immortality.

6 Becoming Gay as an Older Homosexual Man

A free man thinks of nothing less than of death, and his wisdom is not a meditation upon death but upon life.

—SPINOZA

Aging in America is unpleasant. Not only illness and infirmity make it so, but the value placed on youth and beauty do as well. Unlike the cultures of the Far East, which generally revere the aged and often perceive them as possessing unique beauty, our society views age as objectionable and the elderly as unsightly. Here they are usually undervalued, overlooked, and unappreciated.

"Aging homosexuals are doomed to a life of loneliness." This statement, uttered so often by those attempting to dissuade homosexual youth from their sexual orientation, implies that elderly heterosexuals are happier than elderly homosexuals. But six of the eight elderly homosexual men I have seen in psychotherapy have been able to establish mutually loving and stable relationships and to feel more content than at any previous time in their lives. I am defining as "older" or "elderly" a man who is sixty-five years of age or older, a convention that, of course, does not distinguish chronological age from the more valid indicators of aging, such as metabolic and physiological changes.

Adam was in his mid-sixties when he started treatment because of loneliness and depression. He longed to find a lover for the remaining years of his life but was closeted and could not see how this would be possible. A highly articulate and respected attorney, he was raised in a small Southern town, the only child of a well-to-do physician and a mother of striking beauty and charm. Like most men who are homosexual, he had felt different as a child: he had a great appreciation of beauty in art and nature, was more sensitive and emotive than other boys, was not interested in rough-and-tumble sports, and was more drawn to girls than to other boys for companionship.

After Adam's father died when he was ten, he dedicated himself to pleasing his mother. He studied hard, was academically successful, and worked after school to earn extra money.

By the time he was ten or eleven he knew that he was attracted to other boys in his class. As an adolescent whose effusive speech and dramatic gestures were viewed as feminine, he was known as the school "fairy" and sought after by the straight boys for blow jobs. He recounted these episodes humorously, denying any discomfort at being teased and mocked for his feminine manner, although his perturbed tone indicated to me that he had felt deeply humiliated.

The culture of rural America in the early 1940s was even more repressive and unforgiving than today. Adam had little opportunity to take those developmental steps that would have helped him be more affirming of his sexual orientation. As a young adult, he had no gay friends.

He believed that by attempting to be heterosexual he would please his beloved mother, and although his father was by then deceased, that he might finally win the respect of this man who had always seemed too preoccupied to care about him. Although he recognized that he was homosexual in early adolescence, his poor self-regard, the fear of losing his parents' love, and the social opprobrium experienced as an adolescent and young adult had caused Adam to believe that he was perverse and led him to seek professional help on two occasions, once in his late twenties and then in his early forties, to be cured.

After his first therapy he married for the first time. He enjoyed the companionship of his wife and, for a while, their sexual relationship as well, but he continued to have occasional homosexual experiences, which he succeeded in keeping secret from her. His marriage deteriorated over the next fifteen years, ending in an acrimonious divorce.

In the late 1960s he married again, seeking female companionship that, like that of his first wife, reminded him of his adored, now deceased mother. This marriage lasted only a few years and gave him little of the gratification or pleasure that he had found in the early years of his first marriage, since his second wife harassed him for many habits she found irritating. He had, however, continued to keep his occasional homosexual dalliances secret. After he divorced again in the mid-1970s, his sexual activity continued to be limited to brief, mainly anonymous, and usually unsatisfying homosexual encounters. When Adam sought help from me, he was sixty-five, living in New York, and had little social support. He derived some pleasure from occasional sexual encounters but was concerned he would never be able to meet someone with whom he might have a relationship. He was professionally successful but very lonely.

By the end of his first year of therapy, Adam had developed an understanding of his relationship with his parents and how their attitude and that of his peers about his feminine manner and his homosexuality had helped to shape the negative view he held of himself and his sexual orientation. I supported his endeavors to meet other gay men for friendship and sex, though he found it painful to seek these contacts. He also cautiously came out to some straight and gay colleagues at work; he was surprised by their warmth and acceptance.

During his second year of treatment, Adam noticed the attention of a young man in his office who had been especially respectful and conspicuously admiring of him. They began to date and he thoroughly enjoyed the time they spent together, including the sex. About six months later, although concerned about being able to maintain his cherished privacy, he invited his "friend" to live with him.

Feeling that he had derived what he had wanted from treatment, Adam stopped therapy four or five months after his lover moved in. I saw them at a social gathering about two years later. Introducing me to his lover, he said he was soon planning to retire in order to write and travel. He no longer felt lonely or depressed.

It was a surprise to me that after only two years, seeing me only once a week, Adam had been able to make such significant changes in his life. My supporting his efforts to feel positively about being gay, his wish to please me as he had wished to please his parents, the understanding he had gained into the reasons for his low self-regard, and his being psychologically minded had all contributed to his being able to make rapid and significant change. But, most important, the need he felt for love at this late stage of his life provided the motivation for him, as it has for all of my elderly patients, to overcome decades of self-hatred.

For two years I treated a seventy-five-year-old man on a once-weekly basis who had a similarly striking capacity to make good use of therapy late in his life. He wanted an intimate, sexual relationship, but the prospect of such closeness also frightened him. He started to work with me five years after surgery that removed a malignant tumor and two or three months after being told he had been cured.

A formerly successful, now retired banker, John had met Anthony, a man thirty years younger than he, a few months before his surgery. The relationship had never been sexual and had always been a source of anxiety, but after being told he had been cured of his cancer, John became even more anxious about this friendship. His tolerance for pleasure had been greater when time was limited by anticipated death, as had been true for my patients with AIDS. Now, relatively unencumbered by the prospect of immediate death, he was thinking of breaking off the relationship, convinced that Anthony would soon desert him.

John spoke warmly of his parents, who had died many years before, as well as of his older sisters, now in their eighties, who had helped raise him. He had no memory of any trauma, abandonment, or abuse during childhood that might have given meaning to his need to limit life's gratifications, to his social inhibitions or his fear of intimacy. His capacity for recall of early experiences was severely limited, more by denial, I felt, than by any organic deficit of age. He vehemently stated that it was only the cultural attitudes toward same-sex relationships that were responsible for his shame and guilt about his homosexuality; early experiences with family or peers had no bearing on his self-hatred. In his consultation, I had initially thought that his rigid cognitive style and lack of sensitivity to his internal psychological state would make it impossible to engage him in a therapy that might help him to improve his unhappy state. I was wrong!

John was raised in New York City, where he attended public high school and New York University. Although never interested in women, he had had only one or two casual sexual experiences with other boys. He recognized in late adolescence that he was attracted to other men, although he did not think of himself as homosexual but as asexual. He had been socially isolated as an adult, working hard, having a few straight male friends he played cards with regularly, but no intimate relationships. He dated women occasionally but had no sex. Before he met Anthony, he had never had a gay friend or even an acquaintance who was gay—no one with whom he could share either his multiple apprehensions or few pleasures.

He spent most of his hours in therapy ruminating about Anthony's faults, particularly his lack of class, intelligence, and capacity to engage in stimulating conversation. But about six months after we began to work together, largely because of my encouraging him to try, John began to have sex for the first time. He disclaimed any pleasure, proclaiming only how ugly and uncomfortable he had felt without his clothes. Soon thereafter Anthony wanted to move into John's apartment, and my patient, feeling under increasing pressure to have him do so, grew paralyzingly ambivalent and even more ruminative.

I have always been hesitant to give advice to a young patient, not because I believe that it is necessarily clinically incorrect to do so but because it is difficult to know what is going to make him content and happy over an extended period of time or how current circumstances might change over time. I am more likely to respond to the solicitation of advice from an elderly person. It is easier to be able to anticipate the variables that might affect his future simply because time is more limited.

I felt confident responding to John's repeated requests for advice about whether he should permit his lover to move in and suggested that he do so. Anthony was affectionate, took pleasure in caregiving, and appreciated the financial security and comfort that John offered him. My patient needed to be emotionally nurtured and, in the not too distant future, might need physical care, either because of infirmities imposed by age or a recurrence of his cancer. With characteristic and understandable ambivalence, John reluctantly agreed to share his apartment. Like Adam, he adapted readily to the new intimacy and physical proximity, and I was struck by the happiness this new relationship brought him. Although he did stop seeing me soon thereafter, he called me about three years later, asking for a referral to an internist. He informed me that they were still contentedly living together. And John, nearing eighty, was still healthy.

A third man, Harold, sixty-seven when we began to work together, had been living with his lover, twenty-two years his junior, for nearly ten years when he came to see me with some distress about this relationship. He felt that Samuel, his current lover, was not providing him with the affection and support he needed and that his friendships with both men and women were being restricted by Samuel's jealousy. Harold had been in therapy thirty years before with an analyst who was well known for his attempts to convert homosexuals to heterosexuality. He had married three years after completing that treatment, but had left his wife of twenty-four years ten years before seeing me, recognizing that he was gay and wanting to start a new life with a male partner.

Harold's father had ridiculed and humiliated him as a child, probably because he had felt competitive with his son. His mother had been depressed during much of his childhood, frightened of her husband, and emotionally unable to intervene and protect her child from him.

During the course of his once-weekly therapy, he had a passionate affair of many months' duration with a man somewhat younger than his current partner. He said this man made him feel alive and vital. The affair was less problematic and ultimately, he felt, more rewarding than his current relationship, for the younger man was affectionate and made him feel youthful and excited, providing relief from a mild but chronic depression. Through this new relationship he was undoubtedly also expressing anger at Samuel for not providing the love and affection he needed and had been deprived of by his parents.

Perhaps because he had previously been in psychoanalysis and was also quite intelligent, Harold was able to make insightful psychological connections. He grasped quickly how the relationship with his depressed mother had contributed to the difficulty he had loving and feeling loved by Samuel and how he treated Samuel with the same contempt as he had experienced from his abusive father. Harold became more capable of expressing affection as well as aggression, and, no longer feeling impelled to sustain a relationship that he felt to be unsatisfying, he separated from Samuel, devoting himself to his new lover.

Propelled by the need for a revitalizing love at this time in his life, each of these elderly patients was enabled with help to feel more positively about himself and his homosexuality. Each, unencumbered by marriage or vocation, was able to be out and, therefore, in a position to meet other gay men to love and be loved by.

But two of my eight elderly homosexual patients had been heterosexually married for more than forty years when they first sought therapy to become gay. They both wanted to leave their unhappy marriages and to enhance their remaining years by living more authentically. But such a solution to living so many years in a heterosexual lifestyle, although their marriages may not have been satisfying, was not necessarily a healthy or realistic choice at such a late stage of life.

Robert, seventy-four years old with a history of severe hypertension, heart disease, and mild obesity, came to see me to help him pursue a "gay life." He had been married for fifty years. He had been having periodic homosexual encounters since college but was always uncomfortable with being homosexual and had never, until recently, wanted to be gay. He had felt throughout his life that his homosexuality was perverse. Several therapists had encouraged him to enter into and remain in his marriage, which had been asexual for more than thirty years and had never been emotionally gratifying. He was totally closeted socially and within a profession in which he was still active. His wife had no knowledge, he believed, of his homosexual longings.

The specific incident that caused him to see me was the threatened dissolution of a relationship of several years, known to no one, with a younger married man who was planning to leave the city with his family. My patient would meet him about once a month and masturbate him. He was seldom reciprocally touched by this man, who would depart as soon as he had ejaculated. My patient was now frantically trying to find a solution to his anticipated loss, for this sexual partner had been his only connection to a gay life. Although out to no one, my patient had hoped that somehow he would be able to find a new lover with whom he could spend the rest of his life. He intended to leave his wife in order to do so.

After listening to his story for several sessions, I attempted to dissuade him from leaving his spouse. They had children and grandchildren, shared professional interests, property, and emotional bonds that had grown after living so many years together. I believed that the loss would increase his depression and that it would be very difficult for him to find a new lover to take the place of his wife and his sexual partner. He would be better off, I told him, trying to improve his relationship with his wife and gratifying his sexual needs with escorts. This was, I felt, the most realistic though by no means an entirely satisfactory solution to a difficult, life-long problem of being unable to regard himself well or to feel positively about his homosexuality. He was angry, having believed I would advise him to leave his wife. He stopped seeing me after about four months, disgruntled, still married, but, I felt, relieved.

Like those heterosexually married homosexual men of middle age discussed in Chapter 4, Robert needed to repair the discontinuity between his homosexuality and his heterosexual life by attempting to become gay, even at a late age. His need was made urgent by the imminent breakup of his sexual relationship and by life-threatening physical ailments, which increased his fear of death. Making an abrupt change in his life might have helped him to feel that he could live forever, or at least for a much longer time than he could realistically expect. But I felt, in view of his age, health, and current social circumstances, that it would be difficult for him to be out and, therefore, able to find a lover with whom he could share his remaining years. The disintegration of his current life would, I feared, be more debilitating than life-enhancing.

Therapy with the Elderly

Freud was convinced that it was not worthwhile for an analyst to attempt to treat anyone over the age of fifty: "Near or about the fifties the elasticity of the mental process, on which the treatment depends, is as a rule lacking—old people are no longer educable and, on the other hand, the mass of material to be dealt with would prolong the duration of the treatment indefinitely."[1]

Many psychotherapists still believe that major changes are difficult or impossible in mid-life and beyond. This view has caused some not to treat the elderly; thus, lacking experience or knowledge, they find the patients whom they do see difficult to understand. In recent years there has been more interest in defining the specific developmental tasks of old age,[2] but even many therapists who are not psychoanalysts have been biased by Freud's view and prefer to treat younger patients, remaining pessimistic about the therapeutic outcome for the elderly.

As my cases illustrate, many elderly homosexual men have been astonishingly ready to become engaged in therapy that might help them form loving, emotionally gratifying sexual relationships for the first time. Their capacity for coping and adaptation to stress account for some of the ability of these elderly gay men to change and sustain relationships.

Elderly gay men, unlike older heterosexual men, have had to deal throughout their adult lives with social stigmatization and feeling alienated from mainstream culture. Like younger men with HIV and AIDS, they have had more opportunity than most heterosexuals to develop and apply the coping strategies previously learned, enabling them to adapt more effectively to the increasing debility of age and the prejudice directed toward them because they are old.[3] It is probably also true that such capacity for adaptation is not unique to gay men and that anyone who belongs to a minority group that is discriminated against will have learned those coping strategies that enable him to adjust to the stresses of aging and illness more readily than someone who has not been discriminated against.

Some of the developmental challenges for older gay men are similar to those confronting all of the elderly in our society: adapting to deteriorating health, losses, age discrimination, and the fear of death. But there are also important differences. Gay men value maintaining an attractive appearance more than heterosexual men, who often eschew attending to their appearance because it seems narcissistic. It is, however, usually their conviction that it is not masculine to be concerned about appearance that causes straight men to avoid paying appropriate attention to their bodies. Although I believe that the under-valuation of the body and appearance by most heterosexual men is both emotionally and physically unhealthy, those elderly gay men who had previously been able to maintain a youthful appearance and get sexual attention because of it, but are now unable to do so, may lose an important source of self-esteem enhancement.

Although it is true that there is an emphasis on youth and beauty in gay culture, I have also found that a surprising number of young gay men are looking for the emotional warmth, nurture, and comfort provided by an older person, finding the older partner's capacity to offer such emotional security very attractive. Perhaps when AIDS was usually fatal the search for a sense of safety and well-being was more ubiquitous than before. But gay men also long to satisfy a desire for closeness to their father that has so often been thwarted or frustrated in childhood by the father's withdrawal or the child's own anxiety and withdrawal. This longing is obvious in the young man looking for an older partner, but it is also seen in the older man who treats his youthful lover with kindness and care and, identifying with him, gets the love that he longs for himself. This identification with the younger partner's experience is as important a reason for the continued attraction of an older partner to the younger as is the latter's beauty and youth.

Age discrepancy, as well as differences in social status, race, or personality, often provides the emotional tension and excitement for gay men in couples that the difference in gender affords heterosexual couples. These differences usually serve to heighten, enhance, and maintain sexual desire and interest.[4] Complementarity may be even more important in maintaining sexual desire in the elderly than in younger gay men because of the natural physiological mitigation of sexual desire with age.

Elderly gay men may be less inclined than heterosexuals to view age-discrepant relationships as inappropriate, making new sexual relationships seem more possible and therapy more helpful than with elderly heterosexuals. Four of the eight men I have worked with have been enabled to be in relationships for five years or longer with a partner twenty to thirty years younger than they. Of course, I see a relatively affluent sample of gay men, and the more affluent, the more able is any elderly man, gay or straight, to attract a partner, particularly one who is considerably younger. But while it may be the affluence of the older partner that initially attracts a younger man, and the youthful qualities that initially attract the older man to the younger, it appears to be the intrinsic qualities of each, such as loyalty, honesty, and trustworthiness, that make these relationships endure.[5]

HIV has posed more of a health risk for elderly gay men who are sexually active and not appropriately cautious than it does for heterosexual men. HIV/AIDS exists among elderly gay men to a greater extent than commonly acknowledged; for most, AIDS has been a source of significant loss of friends and lovers, making more imminent the specter of their death. The effect of HIV on their lives, even if they were not themselves infected with the virus, caused many to seek therapy, eager to remedy their sense of loss and to find, sometimes for the first time, a committed relationship.

I view the unconscious wish to live forever, however, as the most important reason for the desire for new, loving, passionate relationships in old age, just as it is in middle age. But in the elderly, because of encroaching illness, disability, and the loss of friends, the search for love, as we have seen, may at times be frantic and unrealistic.

"The art of aging creatively," the psychoanalyst Robert Stoller wrote, "lies in one's skill with denial." It is in the service of denial but it is also healthy, he feels, to live as though we can travel on and on, as if we have forever to do so.[6]

By becoming more affirmingly gay and by seeking out a love that nourishes his sense of well-being, an elderly man usually improves his physical health and enhances his emotional health, and may, thereby, perpetuate his life.

Older gay men can contribute significantly to the health and happiness of gay youth.

We read with distressing frequency of the increasing rate of HIV in gay adolescents and young adults.[7] They are now emboldened by the availability of new and effective medical therapies to engage in unsafe sexual practices, and, identifying with self-defeating, self-destructive characteristics of many of the adult gay men who surround them. Many care little about their health. They have adapted to an ethos of dying young.

Role models available to adolescents are too often only celebrities or other adults with HIV or AIDS who have come out. The gay community has had an understandable need to guard the civil rights and enhance the self-regard of HIV-positive gay men, but this need has often been protected at the expense of demonstrating the advantage of living a long life by remaining healthy.[8]

The elderly and others in long-term, committed relationships can demonstrate to those younger and dispirited that they can live long, happy, healthy lives. By becoming models for the value of longevity and love, they can show that aging as a gay man does not destroy the capacity for relationships or intimacy. It is not only important for gay youth that the elderly become such models, it is important for the elderly as well. In this way those who are aging can fight the prejudices of our society that make too many gay men too ready to act in self-destructive ways. For all gay people, fighting hatred is a way to express the rage we may otherwise turn against ourselves:

Coming out is just the first step, the outer coming out. Then we have to start the inner coming out, looking to nourish our own battered self-esteem. And to really be a gay or lesbian citizen, you must also give back to your community. You have to reach out and help it.[9]

7 Opposing Institutional Bias: Anti-Gay Discrimination in Psychoanalysis

For myself, earth-bound and fettered to the scene of my activities, I confess that I do feel the differences of mankind. . . . I am, in plainer words, a bundle of prejudices—made up of likings and dislikings—the veriest thrall to sympathies, apathies, antipathies.

—CHARLES LAMB

On May 9, 1991, the American Psychoanalytic Association issued a statement opposing discrimination in the admission of lesbians and gay men to its affiliated institutes. Almost a year later, on April 23, 1992, the association amended this statement to include the advancement of homosexuals to the positions of training and supervising analyst, the most highly prized and senior training positions within its institutes. The adoption of these statements was the culmination of my eight-year effort to combat the association's longstanding but unwritten policy of excluding those who were openly gay or lesbian from training in its institutes.

In spite of Freud's statement that homosexuals should not be excluded from training to become psychoanalysts,[1] the American Psychoanalytic Association had an unofficial policy that kept men and women who accepted their homosexuality from becoming candidates in their institutes. This policy was based on a theory, held with particular conviction by American psychoanalysts, that homosexuals are fixated at an early stage of development because of inadequate parenting that has interfered with their becoming heterosexual. They are sexual deviants.

The theory that homosexuality is a developmental failure caused by a binding mother or distant father led analysts to assume that all homosexuals have a variety of severe psychological disturbances.[2] As the distinguished British sexologist D. J. West wrote, "Psychoanalysis possesses a considerable repertoire of disagreeable labels, nearly all of them applied sooner or later to homosexuals."[3]

Psychoanalysts were the leading opponents within the American Psychiatric Association of the 1973 decision to delete homosexuality from its *Diagnostic and Statistical Manual.*[4] Opposition to the deletion was articulated by Abram Kardiner, a charter member of the Association for Psychoanalytic Medicine in New York, in a letter to *Psychiatric News:*

> Those who reinforce the disintegrative elements in our society will get no thanks from future generations. The family becomes the ultimate victim of homosexuality, a result which any society can tolerate only within certain limits.
>
> If the American Psychiatric Association endorses one of the symptoms of social distress as a normal phenomenon, it demonstrates to the public its ignorance of social dynamics, of the relation of personal maladaptation to social disharmony, and thereby acquires a responsibility for aggravating the already existing chaos.[5]

An ad hoc committee against the deletion was formed by two analysts, Charles Socarides, a member of the American Psychoanalytic Association who was best known for the passion he brought to his effort to ascribe pathology to homosexuals, and Irving Bieber, who, like Socarides, held the conviction that homosexuality was a treatable mental disorder. Many psychoanalytic societies also unsuccessfully opposed the deletion and wrote as groups to the APA's president that, since homosexuality was a form of "disordered psychosexual development" that was remediable, it should not be removed from the manual.[6]

By the mid-1980s, although most analysts were no longer engaging in such political activity or making bizarre statements about the relationship of homosexuality to social disintegration, they still held tenaciously to the view that homosexuality was a perversion and that all homosexuals were deeply disturbed. As late as 1986, Otto Kernberg, one of America's best-known analysts, wrote, "We just do not find, except very rarely, male homosexuals without significant character pathology."[7]

During the 1980s, homosexuality was still generally considered a treatable symptom. With appropriate therapy over a long period of time that removed their unconscious fears of women, well-motivated homosexuals, analysts believed, could become heterosexual. Those homosexuals who remained sexually active, even if they wanted to become heterosexual, were viewed as difficult patients because they were acting out perverse impulses rather than analyzing them. The more a gay man enjoyed sex, the worse, it was assumed, was his prognosis—the pleasure and gratification of the sexual behavior diminished his motivation to change. Explicit or implicit admonitions were given by such famous analysts as Anna Freud for patients not to act out their sexuality; otherwise, they would lose the therapeutic advantage of their abstinence or attempts at heterosexuality.[8] However, as mentioned in Chapter 3, most harmful to the sense of self-worth of these patients were the often successful efforts analysts made to keep their patients from falling in love, an experience therapists correctly perceived would cause them to value their homosexuality.[9]

Psychoanalysts are taught that the optimal analytic stance is one of neutrality: one does not make value judgments about patients' thoughts, feelings, or behavior. Admonitions to homosexual patients not to have sex obviously did not provide young analysts with a model of neutrality. Until the mid-1980s, therefore, psychoanalysts in training were seldom permitted to analyze those gay men or lesbians who were seeking help but were comfortable with their sexual orientation. They might, however, have been permitted to analyze a patient in conflict about his homosexuality who wanted to become heterosexual, provided he was abstaining from sex.[10]

Freud's theory of childhood sexuality was revolutionary, as was the technique he developed to help his patients recall those childhood fantasies and memories of repressed traumatic experiences that produced symptoms in adulthood. But in order to promote wider acceptance of psychoanalytic theory and to preserve the economic value of the technique, later theorists and practitioners took less radical approaches than their predecessors and eventually became purveyors of traditional social values. Although psychoanalysts have always recognized that human beings have the capacity for a wide range of aggressive and sexual feelings, fantasies, and impulses, the emphasis in clinical practice for the past five or six decades has generally been on patients' containing impulses that do not conform to society's norms and expectations. Masturbation, for example, until about twenty years ago had been viewed by classical analysts as a childhood act, or, at best, an adolescent substitute for and defense against adult vaginal sex. It was seen as a regressive and infantile form of sexual behavior to be avoided in adulthood.[11]

The theory of homosexuality as a developmental deviation, elaborated and codified between 1940 and 1980, enhanced the acceptability of psychoanalysis within mainstream American culture. The theory expressed the bias of the society in which analysts were raised, trained, and worked, and provided the rationalization for keeping lesbian and gay people from being trained in the institutes of the American Psychoanalytic Association.

Since homosexuality was considered an emotional illness, any gay man or lesbian who did not want to be treated for it, but wanted to be a psychoanalyst, was perceived as being either too fearful of traumatic repressed memories or too gratified by perverse sexuality to be analyzable. If unanalyzable, then, ipso facto, he or she would continue to have serious neurotic difficulties that would interfere with his or her ability to analyze others. Therefore, gay men and lesbians who accepted their sexual orientation were not generally accepted for training to be psychoanalysts.

Opposing the bias of the American Psychoanalytic Association was part of my personal and continuing effort to integrate my homosexuality as part of a healthy, positive self-regard. For I continue to believe that any gay man or lesbian who does not oppose the prejudice and discrimination of organizations to which he or she may belong remains enslaved by the self-hatred such institutions engender.

The need to be publicly outspoken about its bias led me in 1983, as chairman of the American Psychoanalytic Association's Program Committee, to organize a panel, "New Perspectives on Homosexuality," with papers by Richard C. Friedman, Stanley Leavy, Robert Stoller, and myself. At a well-attended meeting in December of that year, I argued for a change in both the developmental theory and the clinical treatment of homosexuals and stated that the policy of not training gay men and lesbians was based simply on prejudice, not on an assessment of their capacity to be good analysts. Several analysts walked out. Many, including Charles Socarides, made impassioned rebuttals.[12]

When I submitted a paper, based on my presentation, for publication to *The Journal of the American Psychoanalytic Association,* it was rejected. I had never had an article rejected by that journal, which had previously published two papers and two lengthy reports by me on other analytic subjects. About my article one reader stated that "it would be enough to say that analysts have . . . theoretical misconceptions [about homosexuality] without attributing the results to countertransference." The readers felt that I had not "taken seriously . . . the meanings of homosexuality derived by [other] thoughtful and creative analysts."[13]

At meetings of the association and many psychoanalytic societies over the next three years, I presented the papers that eventually formed the basis for my book *Being Homosexual,* where I attempted to provide a framework for a normal developmental pathway for homosexual men. These ideas were consistently disparaged. In response to one paper a discussant stated in 1985:

> I don't see how it is possible to understand a man's compelling need to love and be loved by other men without understanding its relationship to coexisting conflicts . . . exaggerated fears of intimacy with women, . . . horrifying and highly conflicted unconscious sadistic and masochistic fantasies and wishes of various kinds, . . . denial of castra-

tion, . . . conscious guilt, remorse, expiation and self-punishment.[14]

Another analyst, disagreeing with my views, wrote the same year:

> The homosexual seeks a partner for a number of reparative uses: A) to establish a good mother-child relationship from which he can obtain nurturing supplies; B) to find someone like himself to love as he once wished to be loved; and C) to strive to find his own lost masculinity in the body and the penis of his partner. Since full separation from the mother has not been achieved and identification with the father has been disrupted, he feels incomplete and damaged. . . . Structural change and sexual reorientation are possible to the extent that the analyst can create an atmosphere in which the patient may engage him with his intense disparagement, hate and longing.[15]

A paper on the nature of gay relationships was rejected for presentation at a meeting of the American Psychoanalytic Association because I had attempted to "exonerate or depathologize homosexuality . . . [and] to negate the view that homosexual men are promiscuous."[16]

My attempts to present a normal model for the development of homosexual men led consistently to my colleagues' reiteration of established psychoanalytic developmental and clinical theory. They were unable to acknowledge that their views about homosexuality had been at all influenced by social prejudice. In fact, they were convinced of their own lack of bias, not only because of belief in the scientific validity of the theory but because they thought their own analyses had rid them of such feelings. By 1986 I was persuaded that, like any prejudice, the negative attitudes of most psychoanalysts toward homosexuals were so well rationalized that they could not be overcome by reasoned arguments based on a different clinical and personal perspective. I recognized that if a normal developmental theory and a neutral therapy of gay men were ever to be generally accepted, heterosexual analysts would have to become more familiar with homosexuals outside their office. And this could occur only if there were openly homosexual analysts.

Since the early 1980s I had been out to patients when I felt that not responding to questions about my sexual orientation was harmful to their therapy (see Chapter 2). I was also out to some gay friends, other gay psychiatrists, and my wife. But it was not until 1986 that I began to mention my homosexuality in private discussion of my papers with heterosexual colleagues. I also accepted that year a position on the American Psychiatric Association's Committee on Gay, Lesbian and Bisexual Issues, where my sexual orientation would, I knew, inevitably become known by heterosexual psychiatrists and by psychoanalysts who were active within that organization. From that time and for several years thereafter I was the only openly gay member of the American Psychoanalytic Association.

Each of the several homosexual analysts whom I knew personally or who had seen me in consultation remained closeted. All but one was married, and they were all fearful of the personal, social, and economic stigmatization they would suffer if their sexual orientation became known. One, whom I knew only slightly, became publicly hostile to my views to give credence, I assumed, to his purported heterosexuality. Another, who told me he was bisexual, and with whom I had developed a warm friendship, now avoided speaking to me in professional settings. And a third married, distinguished analyst, who had called me regularly for many years, ceased all social contact.

I was less surprised by the behavior of my heterosexual colleagues. Although before my sexual orientation became known I had continually been referred patients, after I was out I received no further referrals from these same colleagues. One senior analyst, advising his class on the problems of being treated by a homosexual analyst, said that to do so was "like being taught to fly by a blind pilot." Fortunately, by this time I had a practice that had rapidly grown, composed of self-referred gay men, many of whom were themselves mental health professionals wanting therapy or analysis from a gay psychoanalyst.

After the American Psychiatric Association voted in 1973 to delete homosexuality as a mental disorder from its official diagnostic manual, overcoming the formal opposition of most psychoanalysts and analytically oriented psychiatrists, its Board of Trustees endorsed an excellent statement opposing all social and vocational discrimination and criminal sanctions against homosexuals. It said, in part, "Homosexuality per se implies no impairment in judgment, stability, reliability, or general social or vocational capabilities."[17]

Dr. Richard Simons, president of the American Psychoanalytic Association in 1987, had been supportive of my efforts to establish a normal model for the development of homosexual men. I wrote to him on June 7 of that year that it was time for analysts to endorse the American Psychiatric Association's statement opposing discrimination against homosexuals:

> Now, 14 years later . . . at a time when the AIDS epidemic is contributing to increasing discrimination and antigay violence, an endorsement might be of some help. . . . The continuing view of homosexuality as an illness, the ascription of psychopathology to all homosexuals with total disregard of contrary evidence and the prevalent and perni-

cious labeling in our literature and at national meetings of homosexuals as perverts all contribute to prejudice and to the view of gay men and lesbians that psychoanalysts are homophobic.

The Executive Committee of the association refused to endorse the civil rights statement. I assumed it had correctly recognized that the statement had implications with regard both to the established psychoanalytic view of homosexuality as a mental disorder and to the policy of discrimination by its institutes. Instead, the committee asked Simons in November 1987 simply to write the following to the association's Committee on Social Issues:

There are still a great many unresolved questions about the boundaries between the various forms of homosexual behavior and the apparently multiple etiologies that are involved in these various behaviors. The matter of diagnosis of these various forms of homosexual behavior is still controversial, as is the matter of treatment. However it does appear that beyond the scientific considerations there is also a current exacerbation of prejudice and discrimination against homosexual men and women because of the AIDS epidemic. Does the Committee on Social Issues consider it appropriate to recommend a position statement on this aspect of prejudice and discrimination for consideration by the Executive Committee and the Executive Council?

Although a far cry from the American Psychiatric Association's assertion that homosexuals are not psychologically impaired and its call for an end to all discrimination, I thought a statement opposing discrimination against people with AIDS would be a progressive first step. And, for the first time, the organization was officially raising questions about the etiology of homosexuality.

The Committee on Social Issues did prepare a statement that opposed discrimination against homosexuals because of the AIDS epidemic. However, the new president, Homer Curtis of Philadelphia, unlike Richard Simons, was not sympathetic to my efforts to depathologize homosexuality. He asked the committee not to bring up the resolution, asserting that the American Psychoanalytic Association should not take a position on social issues that was not of direct relevance to psychoanalysis.

I assumed that the reason Curtis had asserted the irrelevance of this statement was to avoid the question of institutional discrimination. So I formulated a resolution of more direct relevance to psychoanalysis and psychoanalytic training that he could not avoid taking to the Executive Committee and the Board on Professional Standards:

> The American Psychoanalytic Association deplores all discrimination against persons because of sexual orientation in its affiliated institutes and societies with regard to the admission and progression of candidates and to the appointment and progression of these persons to any position or office.

The Board on Professional Standards considered this statement at its annual meeting but concluded that "a specific resolution was not indicated since the American had been following a nondiscriminating [sic] policy." The association then simply reaffirmed the policy expressed in its bylaws: admission to and progression in training programs should be "based on careful evaluation of personal integrity, analyzability, and educability, not on presumptions based on diagnosis, symptoms, or manifest behavior."

This policy statement had never kept institutes from discriminating against homosexuals. I felt that the decision not to make explicit its opposition to excluding openly gay men and lesbians reflected the association's wish to continue its exclusionist practices as well as its fear that, if such a declaration were made, it could be sued by those who had been rejected in the past or might be rejected in the future.

A few weeks before the board made the decision not to consider my resolution, I had heard from a colleague that two gay men training to become psychiatrists had made informal inquiries to members of the education committees of two separate institutes in New York about the likelihood of their being accepted for psychoanalytic training. Both were told that they should not bother to apply.

One of my friends had been rejected for training many years ago after he had informed an institute that he was homosexual. Determined to become an analyst, he applied to a second institute. This time he did not inform those who interviewed him that he was homosexual. He was accepted. He told his training analyst that he was gay in the privacy of their first session, and his analyst promptly informed the Education Committee. The candidate was asked to withdraw and reapply after he got analyzed. He understood the institute's injunction to mean he should get cured of his homosexuality before reapplying.

I mentioned to Homer Curtis in May 1989 that, because the principles stated in the American Psychoanalytic Association's bylaws had not kept institutes from excluding homosexuals, an explicit resolution was, indeed, needed. He dismissed my comments in a peremptory manner, and I realized that there would be no chance of the association's disavowing discrimination while he was the president.

When I had been on committees of both the American Psychoanalytic and International Psychoanalytical associations, I had been surprised to discover how invested analysts were in maintaining a good public image. The American Psychoanalytic Association particularly disliked negative publicity about internal squabbles and theoretical differences that led to occasional but often acrimonious disputes within and between its institutes, believing that any appearance of organizational instability could discourage patients from turning to psychoanalysts for treatment.

I decided, therefore, that some public comment might prompt the association to reconsider its position on training homosexuals. In May 1989 I wrote to *Psychiatric News,* the official newspaper of the American Psychiatric Association, of my unsuccessful attempts to get the American Psychoanalytic Association either to endorse the APA's 1973 statement opposing public discrimination or to oppose discrimination toward openly lesbian and gay people in their training institutes.

At the time, *Psychiatric News* had a circulation of about 35,000; it was sent to all psychiatrists, who were an important source of analysts' patient referrals, and to physicians training to be psychiatrists, from whom the American Psychoanalytic Association then drew most of its candidates for training. Since I was then a member of the American Psychiatric Association's Committee on Gay, Lesbian and Bisexual Issues, I was confident that the APA would be sympathetic to my concern. Furthermore, there were prominent people in the APA, both homosexual and heterosexual, who remained resentful of organized psychoanalysis and of individual analysts like Socarides, who had so vehemently opposed removing homosexuality from the diagnostic manual of mental disorders.

Psychiatric News did an extensive article in its July 21, 1989, issue. When he was interviewed for the article, Homer Curtis denied that the association had a policy of excluding gay applicants but did acknowledge that admission decisions were left up to each training institute, which "may believe that a homosexual may be unanalyzable and uneducable." Judd Marmor, a former APA president instrumental in the 1973 decision to delete homosexuality from the diagnostic manual, was quoted as stating that the American Psychoanalytic Association's refusal to condemn discrimination was "disgraceful" and a "continuation of a well-known discriminatory practice that has no scientific justification."[18]

Within three months after the appearance of the article, the Executive Committee of the American Psychoanalytic Association endorsed the APA's 1973 position statement on homosexuality and civil rights. Dr. Curtis wrote a letter to all members of the association and to *Psychiatric News* of this decision.[19] However, he continued to deny that there was any discrimination against homosexuals in its institutes, and the association continued to refuse to discuss my request for a resolution that explicitly opposed such discrimination.

Following the publication of the article, the American Academy of Psychoanalysis, an organization of analysts not affiliated with the American Psychoanalytic Association, issued a statement condemning discrimination against homosexuals. Although the academy has no training function, it passed a resolution opposing "an applicant's sexual orientation as grounds for rejecting him or her from any educational or vocational institution."[20]

Shortly thereafter, James Marks, one of the cooperating attorneys of the ACLU's Gay and Lesbian Projects Division, had been told of possible discrimination against a homosexual candidate applying for admission to the Boston Psychoanalytic

Institute. He wrote to the institute, which responded by incorporating into its bylaws a statement opposing discrimination on the basis of sexual orientation.

The American Psychoanalytic Association by this time had a new, more progressive president, George Allison. I spoke with him informally by telephone in October 1990 about the inherent cruelty and injustice of discrimination and then wrote reminding him that, in addition to the unfairness, "many institutes are in communities that have ordinances that make discrimination on the basis of sexual orientation illegal." I asked him to take the following statement to the Executive Committee, which William Rubenstein, director of the ACLU's Gay and Lesbian Projects Division, had informally helped me prepare:

> No affiliate institute of the American Psychoanalytic Association shall exclude or . . . otherwise discriminate against any person seeking admission to or advancement within such institutes . . . nor deny advancement to or the benefits of faculty status or supervising or training analyst status on the basis of a person's sexual orientation.

In March 1991, Dr. Allison did take the resolution to a meeting of the Executive Committee, which by then knew of the disavowal of discriminatory practices by both the Academy of Psychoanalysis and the Boston Psychoanalytic Institute. Although the committee revised my statement, omitting the right to attain training and supervisory status, it did draft a resolution that for the first time specifically stated that sexual orientation should not be considered in evaluating candidates for admission for training. The official statement was approved by the Executive Committee in May 1991.

Psychiatric News reported the adoption of this resolution of nondiscrimination, quoting Allison that "considerable enlightenment" had occurred throughout the American Psychoanalytic Association on issues related to homosexuality. In a forthright statement he also said that members were taking a closer look at the politics and sociology of homosexuality as well as at the increasing evidence of a biological component to sexual orientation and that "increasing understanding has diminished homophobic attitudes that clouded some analysts' views of homosexuality."[21]

The adoption of the resolution was very important. I remained troubled, however, that the right to become a training and supervising analyst had been specifically omitted at the request of the Board on Professional Standards. The board is in charge of training standards and is its most consistently conservative body; the majority of its members opposed allowing openly homosexual persons to supervise and analyze candidates in training.

I objected to this decision in a letter to Dr. Allison on March 18, 1991, and in his response he acknowledged that there had been "organizational difficulties" in having the statement elaborated to include training analysts. From my point of view this was not simply an equal rights issue. The refusal of the Board on Professional Standards to have homosexual training analysts was indicative, I believed, of its continuing conviction that a homosexual person could not be as good an analyst as a heterosexual. Any official statement that gave the impression that homosexual people might not be as competent as heterosexuals could deter analysts from endorsing clinical and developmental theories that depathologized homosexuality. I also believed that, if the American Psychoanalytic Association did state that analysis and supervision of candidates could be done by openly homosexual people, it would be difficult for analysts and other clinicians to continue to maintain that homosexuals should try to become heterosexual in order to function optimally.

I called the chairman of the Board on Professional Standards, Marvin Margolis, in August 1991 to discuss the exclusion of training analysts in the resolution. He was interested in my own experience in analysis and asked me whether I wanted to become a training analyst. He appeared to believe that I had wanted training and supervising analysts included in the statement because I had not been appointed one. I assured him that, although earlier in my career I had wanted to be a training analyst, I was now too busy with other obligations and had no such interest. He then abruptly concluded the conversation, asking that I write him a formal letter for consideration by the board. I wrote him on August 13, 1991, but he did not respond to my letter. Then I left a message on his answering machine, which he did not return. Before the association's December 1991 meeting I asked the administrative director to make certain Margolis had received my letter, which she confirmed. I asked her to remind him to respond. And he still did not.

Frustrated and angry, I again asked William Rubenstein of the American Civil Liberties Union for help. He agreed to write a letter to the officers of the association, but in order to do so the ACLU had to have a client. On April 23, 1992, on behalf of both the National Lesbian and Gay Health Foundation, a large organization of gay and lesbian health professionals on whose Board of Directors I served, and the American Medical Students Association, the ACLU wrote to express concern that training and supervising analysts had been excluded in the position statement. He reminded them that "this omission is illogical, inconsistent, and in many of the localities in which the Association has psychoanalytic institutes, including New York City, illegal."

The Executive Committee acted swiftly, and one week later the American Psychoanalytic Association approved an amended statement that included training and supervising analysts.[22] The amended resolution implied that homosexuals, like heterosexuals, had the emotional health, psychological insight, and ability not only to be psychoanalysts but to analyze and train other analysts.

In his comments to *Psychiatric News,* Margolis stated: "The earlier statement was in fact intended to cover all faculty as well as trainees . . . despite no specific mention of the training and supervising analysts. The recent extension of the antidiscrimination policy only corrects an oversight in its wording and is not in response to the protest by the ACLU."[23]

Recent Developments

A group of psychoanalysts and other clinicians led by Charles Socarides were distressed by the American Psychoanalytic Association's resolution as well as by an article I had published in *Psychiatric News* in which I inveighed against attempts by many analytically oriented therapists to change homosexuals to heterosexuals.[24] They formed the National Association for Research and Therapy of Homosexuality (NARTH), whose aims included countering the impression that homosexuality was a normal variant of human sexuality.[25]

In 1992 Socarides also helped to organize the Committee of Concerned Psychoanalysts within the American Psychoanalytic Association, a group that wanted the membership to be clear about "whether or not homosexuals who are candidates in training would be analyzed for their homosexuality [and] whether homosexuality is now considered a normal form of sexual behavior."[26] They made an unsuccessful attempt to overturn the new position statement by referendum.

In December 1992, the association appointed an Ad Hoc Committee on Issues of Homosexuality to assist the membership in becoming "aware of the results of bias and discrimination that may persist and to facilitate appropriate changes in attitudes and in policy." The committee had the important function of attempting "to end bias and discrimination, within institutes," but it had no mandate to attempt to resolve any differences of opinion that affected the clinical care of homosexuals, such as whether homosexuality is a sexual deviation caused by poor parenting or a normal variant of human sexuality, or whether sexual orientation can be changed by psychoanalysis.[27]

The committee's chairman attempted to bring together a consensus for its work partly by minimizing the past history of the American Psychoanalytic Association with regard to discrimination. Shortly before he was named chairman, he wrote in reference to the recently adopted antidiscrimination statements: "There has, of course, been pressure to adopt such a statement, beginning about twenty years ago; but it has come from our own members and from our Committee on Social Issues."[28]

Negative publicity and threat of a lawsuit had been responsible for the increasing understanding of analysts that exclusion of homosexuals from training had been based on bias and not on evidence of their inability to function as analysts. Nevertheless, on May 20, 1993, in order to placate those who had been vociferous in their opposition to the statement opposing bias, the Executive Council passed yet another resolution, approved by the membership: "The contract entered into by analyst and analysand is a private one. Once embarked in a treatment, the goals are the concern of the patient and analyst only."[29] This statement continues to carry the unfortunate implication that attempts to change homosexual people to heterosexual, including an openly gay candidate in training, remain an acceptable modality of treatment. Analysts still either do not understand or choose to overlook what is well known to those like myself and many of my patients who have been subjected to such therapies: efforts to change a homosexual to a heterosexual, even if the patient desires such a change, often cause psychological damage.

The institutes of the American Psychoanalytic Association have started to accept a few openly gay and lesbian candidates for training. But in this period of change and transition from a pathological to a normal developmental model, there is little teaching at all about homosexuality. The analysis and supervision of the few gay and lesbian candidates now being trained are generally done by an older generation of heterosexual analysts who are trying to learn, but are not knowledgeable, about the development of gay men and lesbians. And, as Richard C. Friedman and Jennifer Downey, analysts who have done research in the area of sexual orientation, noted in 2002: "Our impression is that many psychoanalysts throughout the world presently hold mutually contradictory beliefs about homosexuality. This presumably has an influence on clinical practice."[30]

Until his death in 2005, Charles Socarides held seminars on homosexuality at annual meetings of the American Psychoanalytic Association; a group of distinguished senior analysts in New York until recently met monthly to discuss the progress of their homosexual patients in achieving heterosexuality through the analysis of their early conflicts. In a lecture sponsored by the Psychoanalytic Center of California in January 1995, Otto Kernberg, who was subsequently president of the International Psychoanalytical Association, presented his view that many homosexuals can be changed to heterosexuals, and that analysts "should be able to stand up against politically correct thinking." He added that "the analyst has to proceed from a position of technical neutrality."[31] And the National Association for Research and Therapy of Homosexuality (NARTH) currently meets annually to present papers and to train therapists to change homosexuals to heterosexuals. Although most mental health professionals now accept that society's prejudice does harm to the mental health and emotional well-being of homosexuals and most no longer believe that homosexuals can be changed to heterosexuals, there is clearly more work to be done.

The clinical position still held by some psychoanalysts, and other clinicians as well, that homosexuals have a perverse sexual orientation that can be changed is used by the political right and conservative religious denominations to oppose legal efforts by homosexuals to fight the discrimination that deprives us of the same civil rights as heterosexuals. If homosexuals are capable of being heterosexual, it is argued, then they need treatment, not equal rights. The same point is used to oppose the right of gay people to choose to be married. However, underlying the opposition to gay men and lesbians in committed relationships is also society's need to support its prejudice by maintaining that homosexuals are different, promiscuous, antifamily, and antisocial.

Opposing discrimination in a prejudiced society is good for the psyche. It directs anger away from ourselves to where it rightfully belongs. But it is love that makes us know who we are. And let no individual, no organization, and no institution try to take that away!

NOTES

Introduction: Being Homosexual and Becoming Gay

1. In the 1970s, following the American Psychiatric Association's decision to remove homosexuality from its *Diagnostic and Statistical Manual of Disorders,* and building on Evelyn Hooker's groundbreaking study, "The Adjustment of the Male Overt Homosexual" (*Journal of Projective Techniques* [1957], 21:18–31), a few analytically oriented therapists had begun to question the psychoanalytic theory of male homosexuality. Notable among them were Frank Lachman, "Homosexuality: Some Diagnostic Perspectives and Dynamic Considerations," *American Journal of Psychotherapy* (1975), 29:254–60; John Gonsiorek, "Psychological Adjustment and Homosexuality," *Social and Behavioral Sciences Documents, MS 1478* (San Rafael, Calif.: Select Press, 1977); and Stephen Mitchell, "Psychodynamics, Homosexuality and the Question of Pathology," *Psychiatry* (1978), 41:254–63. More elaborate and more critical appraisals of the theory were made in the 1980s: Robert Friedman, "The Psychoanalytic Model of Male Homosexuality: A Historical and Theoretical Critique," *Psychoanalytic Review* (1986), 73(4):483–519; Richard C. Friedman, *Male Homosexuality: A Contemporary Psychoanalytic Perspective* (New Haven: Yale University Press, 1988); Kenneth Lewes, *Homosexuality and Psychoanalysis* (New York: Simon & Schuster, 1988); and my earlier book, *Being Homosexual: Gay Men*

and Their Development (New York: Farrar, Straus & Giroux, 1989).

2. Robert Bak, "Object Relations in Schizophrenia and Perversion," *International Journal of Psycho-analysis* (1971), 52:235–42.

3. Abram Kardiner, "The Social Distress Syndrome of Our Time, I," *Journal of the American Academy of Psychoanalysis* (1978):89–101.

4. Franz Kallmann, "A Comparative Twin Study on the Genetic Aspects of Male Homosexuality," *Journal of Nervous and Mental Disease* (1952), 15:283–98; Elke Eckert et al., "Homosexuality in Monozygotic Twins Reared Apart," *British Journal of Psychiatry* (1986), 148:421–25; and Richard Pillard and James Weinrich, "Evidence of Familial Nature of Male Homosexuality," *Archives of General Psychiatry* (1986), 43:808–12.

5. Richard Green studied forty-four "feminine" boys and found that about two-thirds became homosexual or bisexual adults. One cannot infer from his studies what percentage of homosexual adults were unconventionally male as boys, but my clinical impression from my adult patients is about the same as his empirical observation. See Richard Green, *The "Sissy Boy Syndrome" and the Development of Homosexuality* (New Haven: Yale University Press, 1987).

6. Although my clinical observations had convinced me of the constitutional nature of homosexuality, they did not, of course, prove that it is biological in origin. Empirical studies published after my book, however, lend further credence both to the biological basis of homosexuality in men and to its having a genetic determinant as well: Simon Le Vay, "A Difference in Hypothalamic Structure Between Heterosexual and Homosexual Men," *Science* (1991), 253:1034–37. Le Vay discusses his work and other biological studies of sexual behavior and feelings in *The Sexual Brain* (Cambridge: MIT Press, 1993); see also Laura Allen and Roger Gorski, "Sexual Orientation and the Size of the Anterior Commissure in the Human Brain," *Proceedings of the National Academy of Science* (1992), 89:7199–202. The hypothesis that homosexuality is genetically determined is supported by the study of J. Michael Bailey and Richard Pillard, "A Genetic Study

of Male Sexual Orientation," *Archives of General Psychiatry* (1991), 48:1089–93, and by the important studies of Dean Hamer, Stella Hu, et al., "A Linkage Between DNA Markers on the X Chromosome and Male Sexual Orientation," *Science* (1993), 261:321–27, and "Linkage Between Sexual Orientation and Chromosome xq28 in Males but Not in Females," *Nature Genetics* (1995), 11:248–56. In *The Science of Desire* (New York: Simon & Schuster, 1994), Dean Hamer and Peter Copeland elaborate on Hamer's discovery of a gene marker linked to male homosexuality. There is an interesting review of the books by Le Vay and by Hamer and Copeland by Richard Horton, "Is Homosexuality Inherited?" *The New York Review of Books* (July 13, 1995), 52:12, 36–41. Also see Glenn Wilson and Qazi Rahman, *Born Gay: The Psychobiology of Sex Orientation* (London: Peter Owen, 2005).

7. K. J. Dover, *Greek Homosexuality* (New York: Vintage Books, 1978), esp. pp. 6–111. In his last book, the historian John Boswell documents that these formal relationships between an older "lover" and younger "beloved" were not the only type of homosexual relationships in ancient Greece, where there was greater variety than this traditional view implies; see *Same-Sex Unions in Premodern Europe* (New York: Villard, 1994), pp. 56–57, 71–72.

8. Gilbert Herdt, *The Sambia: Ritual and Gender in New Guinea* (New York: Holt, Rinehart & Winston, 1987).

9. For more detailed discussion of becoming gay, or "homosexual identity formation," see Vivian Cass, "Homosexual Identity Formation: A Theoretical Model," *Journal of Homosexuality* (1979), 4:219–35, and her interesting paper on "The Implications of Homosexual Identity Formation for the Kinsey Model and Scale of Sexual Preference," in *Homosexuality/Heterosexuality,* edited by D. P. McWhirter, S. A. Sanders, and J. M. Reinisch (New York: Oxford University Press, 1990). See also Eli Coleman's discussion of the "Developmental States in the Coming out Process," *Journal of Homosexuality* (1981), 7:31–43. For narratives of coming out by youth in Chicago, see Gilbert Herdt and Andrew Boxer, *Children of Horizons* (Boston: Beacon Press, 1993),

in which the authors discuss and compare the social and developmental significance of the coming-out process for gay and lesbian adolescents from varied ethnic and social backgrounds.

10. Paul Monette, "The Politics of Silence," *The New York Times,* March 7, 1993.

Chapter 1: Becoming Gay: A Personal Odyssey

1. The technique of free association grew out of Freud's frustration with the transitory benefit of removing symptoms by hypnotic suggestion. He recognized that improvement with hypnosis was brought about solely by the patient's desire to please the physician and was apt to fade when contact was withdrawn. In the case of Elizabeth Von R., whom he treated in 1892, he dispensed with hypnosis and used concentration alone, asking his patient to recall memories that might elucidate her symptoms. Between 1892 and 1895, free association gradually replaced the cathartic method as the preferred technique for recollecting early traumatic memories. But there are remnants of suggestion in all analyses, i.e., in the repetition of interpretations daily over many years. See Ernest Jones, *The Life and Work of Sigmund Freud,* Vol. 1 (New York: Basic Books, 1953), p. 240.

2. Since the late 1960s there had been an informal gay association that met secretly during the annual convention of the American Psychiatric Association. By 1973 a caucus of gay and lesbian psychiatrists had been formed to help gay and lesbian members of the association become more open. By 1979, the caucus had about seventy-five members and was called the Association of Gay and Lesbian Psychiatrists. An official APA Committee on Gay, Lesbian and Bisexual Issues was formed that same year. I was a member of that committee from 1986 to 1993 and its chairperson from 1991 to 1993. See Ronald Bayer, *Homosexuality and American Psychiatry* (New York: Basic Books, 1981), pp. 162–78.

3. The panelists were Stanley Leavy, Robert Stoller, Richard C. Friedman, and myself. The report on this panel was written by Richard C. Friedman and published as "Toward a Further

Understanding of Homosexual Men," in *Journal of the American Psychoanalytic Association* (1986), 34:193–206.

Chapter 2: The Gay Therapist

1. For further discussion of how the bias in psychoanalytic theory has affected the treatment of gay men, see my article, "On the Analytic Therapy of Homosexual Men," *Psychoanalytic Study of the Child* (1985), 40:235–54, and my earlier book, *Being Homosexual: Gay Men and Their Development* (New York: Farrar, Straus & Giroux, 1989), pp. 3–23, 109–27. Also see Jack Drescher, *Psychoanalytic Theory and the Gay Man* (Hillside, NJ: The Analytic Press, 1998), and Richard C. Friedman and Jennifer I. Downey, *Sexual Orientation and Psychodynamic Psychotherapy* (New York: Columbia, 2002), pp. 284–90.

2. I wrote *Being Homosexual* to define a normal path of development for gay men, in distinction to the analytic view of deviant development. But I maintain the traditional psychoanalytic perspective of the importance of childhood experiences and the unconscious in understanding adult behavior.

3. Here are but a few examples of this point of view: Lawrence Kolb and Adelaide Johnson, "Etiology and Therapy of Overt Homosexuality," *Psychoanalytic Quarterly* (1953), 24:506–16; Irving Bieber et al., *Homosexuality* (New York: Basic Books, 1962); and Charles Socarides, *Homosexuality* (New York: Jason Aronson, 1978).

4. Sigmund Freud (1937), "Analysis Terminable and Interminable" (London: Hogarth Press, 1964), *Standard Edition* 23:248.

5. See *Being Homosexual,* pp. 109–27.

Chapter 3: The Homosexual Adolescent

1. For example, see Peter Blos, *On Adolescence* (New York: Free Press, 1962), p. 143; Selma Fraiberg, "Homosexual Conflicts," in *Adolescence: Psychoanalytic Approach to Problems and Therapy,* edited by S. Lorand and H. I. Schneer (New York: Paul E. Hober, 1961), pp. 78–112; Moses Laufer, "The Body Image: The

Function of Masturbation and Adolescence," *Psychoanalytic Study of the Child* 23 (1968):114–37; Leo Spiegel, "Comments on the Psychoanalytic Psychology of Adolescence," *Psychoanalytic Study of the Child* 13 (1958).

2. See Fraiberg, "Homosexual Conflicts"; also Moses Laufer and M. Eglé Laufer, "Why Psychoanalytic Treatment for These Adolescents?" in *Developmental Breakdown and Psychoanalytic Treatment in Adolescence,* edited by M. Laufer and M. E. Laufer (New Haven: Yale University Press, 1989).

3. See Simon Le Vay, *The Sexual Brain* (Cambridge: MIT Press, 1993), pp. 71–138; "Viewpoint," *The Advocate* (March 21, 1995): 49; and *Queer Science* (Cambridge: MIT Press, 1996). Also see Glenn Wilson and Qazi Rahman, op. cit, chap. 7.

4. For elaboration of the nature of the relationship of a homosexual child with his father, see my article, "Fathers and Their Homosexually Inclined Sons in Childhood," *Psychoanalytic Study of the Child* 41 (1986); *Being Homosexual* (New York: Farrar, Straus & Giroux, 1989), chap. 3; and *Commitment and Healing,* op. cit, Chapters 1 & 2.

5. Fraiberg, "Homosexual Conflicts."

6. Ibid., p. 83.

7. Ibid., p. 78. Like Fraiberg, the Laufers view psychoanalysis in adolescence as enabling the adolescent to believe that there is "possibility of a life other than an abnormal one . . . an established perversion." In speaking of homosexual adolescents in need of help, they comment, "Puberty and adolescence confronted them unconsciously with the reality of their failed sexual bodies." They too see homosexuality as a developmental foreclosure, a psychic surrender. Laufer and Laufer, "Why Psychoanalytic Treatment for These Adolescents?" pp. 21–22.

8. Fraiberg, "Homosexual Conflicts," p. 102.

9. As Paul's comfort with his sexuality and intimacy increased, he became more interested in and had greater opportunity for more intimate forms of sexual expression, including anal sex. In working with Paul as an adolescent and young adult, as in working with any patient today, I do not hesitate to educate about safe-sex

guidelines. For further information about educating adolescents and young adults about safe sex, see *Being Homosexual,* chap. 5; Gary Remafedi, "Preventing the Sexual Promiscuity of AIDS During Adolescence," *Journal of Adolescent Health Care* (1988), 9(1):39–143; and M. Rotheram-Borus, C. Koopman, and A. Erhardt, "Homeless Youths and HIV Infection," *American Psychologist* (1991), 46(11):1188–97. Also Walt Odets, "Why We Stopped Doing Primary Prevention for Gay Men in 1985," *Aids and Public Policy Journal* (1995), 10(1):1–29.

10. Peter Blos, *Fathers and Sons* (New York: International Universities Press, 1985), p. 50.

11. The adolescent with a bisexual nature, unlike the homosexual adolescent, gets a good deal of gratification from his heterosexual relationships, usually chooses to suppress his homosexual impulses, and is able to do so comfortably.

12. Blos, *Fathers and Sons,* pp. 3–55.

13. For a review of the literature on gay and lesbian youth and for their suggestions on the direction of future research, see Andrew Boxer, Bertram Cohler, Gilbert Herdt, and Floyd Irvin, "Gay and Lesbian Youth," in *Handbook on Clinical Research and Practice with Adolescents* (New York: Wiley, 1993). In *Children of Horizons* (Boston: Beacon Press, 1993), Gilbert Herdt and Andrew Boxer discuss how age, sex, class, and ethnic group affect the coming-out process.

14. Most adolescents who self-identify in early adolescence, at ages eleven, twelve, or thirteen, have been forced to do so because they are gender atypical or noticeably unconventional in other ways. Many have been rejected by their parents and peers. Social agencies such as the Hettrick-Martin Institute in New York and Project Ten in California provide special schooling and counseling for this group of unconventional gay youth and have been helpful in countering the effects of rejection and social stigmatization.

15. The suicide rate in gay and lesbian youth is estimated to be about 25 percent of all adolescent suicides. In one study, 30 percent of 137 gay or bisexual adolescent boys said they had attempted suicide. It is most likely among adolescents who are the most

gender-nonconforming and, therefore, most frequently rejected and stigmatized that this rate is the highest. See Gary Remafedi, *Pediatrics* (1991), 87:869–75. Also see Paul Gibson, "Gay Male and Lesbian Youth Suicide," in *Report of the Secretary's Task Force on Youth Suicide,* Vol. 3 (Washington, D.C.: Department of Health and Human Services, August 1989).

16. See Walt Odets, "Psychosocial and Educational Challenges for the Gay and Bisexual Male Communities," paper delivered at the AIDS Prevention Summit, American Association of Physicians for Human Rights, Dallas, Texas, July 15–17, 1994; and his publication "Why We Stopped Doing Primary Prevention for Gay Men in 1985."

17. Parents who seek consultation with me want to offer their children a stable and affirming environment. Those who would be more critical of their adolescent for his homosexuality or who want him to attempt to change his sexual orientation would seek consultation elsewhere. Therefore, I am seeing a skewed population of both parents and adolescents.

18. See my article, "The Second Separation Stage of Adolescence," in *The Course of Life,* edited by Stanley Greenspan and George Pollock, Vol. 3 (New York: International Universities Press, 1993), pp. 453–68.

Chapter 4: The Dilemma of Heterosexually Married Homosexual Men

1. Surveys conducted in the United States, the Netherlands, Denmark, and West Germany between 1974 and 1981 indicated that at the time 15 to 20 percent of all homosexual men were or had been married. See Michael W. Ross, *The Married Homosexual Man* (London: Routledge & Kegan Paul, 1983), pp. 20–24. Most likely, fewer homosexual men are marrying now than when these surveys were conducted because there is greater social tolerance for same-sex relationships.

2. The analyst Robert Liebert opined that for homosexual men in the time of AIDS, "in terms of survival it is advantageous to be [married and] heterosexual." See his article, "Middle-Aged

Homosexual Men: Issues in Treatment," in *The Middle Years,* edited by John M. Oldham and Robert Liebert (New Haven: Yale University Press, 1989), p. 158.

3. In Chapter 8 of *Being Homosexual* (New York: Farrar, Straus & Giroux, 1989), I discuss the role that the unanalyzed transference wish for a father's love plays in "conversion" or "reparative" therapies and most analyses of homosexual men.

4. André Gide, *Madeleine* (Chicago: Elephant Paperbacks/Ivan R. Dee, 1989), pp. 21–23.

5. See Laud Humphreys, *The Tea Room Trade: Impersonal Sex in Public Places* (Chicago: Aldine Press, 1970). Fifty-four percent of the sample of men Humphreys surveyed who were engaging in sex in rest rooms were married and living with their wives.

6. For a good discussion of adjustment and development in the second half of life, see Bertram Cohler and Robert Galatzer-Levy, "Self, Meaning and Morale Across the Second Half of Life," in *New Dimensions in Adult Development,* edited by Robert Nemeroff and Calvin Colarusso (New York: Basic Books, 1990), pp. 214–60.

7. For an excellent article on the therapy of gay men with self-esteem injury, see Carlton Cornett, "Dynamic Psychotherapy of Gay Men: A View from Self Psychology," in *Affirmative Dynamic Psychotherapy with Gay Men,* edited by Carlton Cornett (Northvale, N.J.: Jason Aronson, 1993), pp. 45–76.

8. Catherine Whitney, *Uncommon Lives: Gay Men and Straight Women* (New York: New American Library, 1990), p. 154.

9. Ibid., pp, 154–55.

10. See Glenn Wilson and Qazi Rahman, op. cit, pp. 16–22.

11. I discuss the topic of bisexuality more fully and give a brief clinical history of this patient in *Being Homosexual,* pp. 103–108.

12. See Calvin Colarusso and Robert Nemeroff, "Clinical Implications of Adult Developmental Theory," *American Journal of Psychiatry* (October 1987), 144(10):1263–70, for a succinct discussion of their view of adult development.

13. Daniel J. Levinson et al., *The Seasons of Men's Life* (New York: Ballantine Books, 1979), p. 328.

Chapter 5: Developing a Postive Gay Identity with HIV or AIDS

1. See *Psychiatric Dictionary,* edited by Robert J. Campbell, 6th ed. (New York: Oxford University Press, 1989), p. 785.

2. Rates of major depressive disorders are similar in a population of HIV-positive and HIV-negative homosexual men and in the general population. See D. Ostrow, A. Monjan, and J. Joseph, "HIV-Related Symptoms and Psychological Functioning in a Cohort of Homosexual Men," *American Journal of Psychiatry* (1989), 146:737–42.

3. The following articles discuss the benefits of counseling for these patients: Samuel Perry and John Markowitz, "Counseling for HIV Testing," *Hospital and Community Psychiatry* (July 1988), 39(7):731–39; John Markowitz, Gerald Klerman, and Samuel Perry, "Interpersonal Psychotherapy of Depressed HIV-Positive Outpatients," *Hospital and Community Psychiatry* (September 1992), 43(9):885–90; John Markowitz, Judith Rabkin, and Samuel Perry, "Treating Depression in HIV-Positive Patients," *AIDS* (1994), 8:403–12.

4. Gordon W. Allport, *Becoming* (New Haven: Yale University Press, 1955), p. 87.

5. Markowitz, Klerman, and Perry noted that "the shared recognition that time was precious galvanized both our patients and us, intensified a mutual engagement and commitment and led to surprisingly dramatic interpersonal changes" ("Interpersonal Psychotherapy of Depressed HIV-Positive Outpatients," p. 889).

6. For a discussion of the relationship between self-esteem injury and masochistic inclinations, see Arnold Cooper, "The Unusually Painful Analysis: A Group of Narcissistic-Masochistic Characters in Psychoanalysis," in *Psychoanalysis: The Vital Issues,* edited by George Pollock and John Gedo, Vol. 2 (New York: International Universities Press, 1984). Also see his article, "Narcissism and Masochism," *Psychiatric Clinics of North America* (September 1989), 12(3):541–52.

7. For references to these earliest articles on AIDS, see Jeanne Kassler,

Gay Men's Health (New York: Harper & Row, 1983), pp. 35, 150–53.

8. Dr. John Markowitz wrote:

> Gay men, heterosexuals, IV drug users and women infected with HIV often seem to discover the capacity to change their lives and relationships, to live out fantasies in what might be the last gasp of their lives. Some drug users have said, "Getting infected was the best thing that ever happened to me; without HIV I never would have quit using." Not everyone reacts this way, of course, but those who show up for therapy may be desperately willing to use HIV as an epiphany, as a galvanizing force in their lives [personal communication].

See also Markowitz, Klerman, and Perry, "Interpersonal Psychotherapy of Depressed HIV-Positive Outpatients."

9. In *Archives of General Psychiatry* (February 1991), 48:111–19, Judith Rabkin, Jane Williams, Robert Remien, et al. report that there is no significant correlation in HIV-positive men between depression and the amount of immunosuppression or degree of advanced illness. In another article they found "high levels of hope and low levels of . . . depressive symptoms" in a selected group of well-educated homosexual men. See "Maintenance of Hope in HIV Spectrum Homosexual Men," *American Journal of Psychiatry* (October 1990), 147(10):1322–26. F. Patrick McKegney and Mary Alice O'Dowd reported that 322 patients with AIDS were significantly less suicidal than 82 who were HIV-infected but without AIDS. See "Suicidality and HIV Status," *American Journal of Psychiatry* (March 1992), 149(3):96–98.

10. See Robert Nemiroff and Calvin Colarusso, eds., *New Dimensions in Adult Development* (New York: Basic Books, 1990), p. 106.

11. Irving Yallom and C. Greaves, "Group Therapy with the Terminally Ill," *American Journal of Psychiatry* (1977), 134:396–400.

Chapter 6: Becoming Gay as an Older Homosexual Man

1. Sigmund Freud (1905 [1904]), "On Psychotherapy" (London: Hogarth Press, 1953), *Standard Edition* 7:264.

2. See, for example, S. H. Cath and C. Cath, "The Race Against Time," in *Psychotherapy and Psychoanalysis in the Second Half of Life,* edited by Robert Nemiroff and Calvin Colarusso (New York: Plenum, 1984), pp. 241–62. See also Bertram Cohler and Robert Galatzer-Levy, "Self-meaning and Morale Across the Second Half of Life," in *New Dimensions in Adult Development,* edited by Robert Nemiroff and Calvin Colarusso (New York: Basic Books, 1990), pp. 214–60; and the two-volume work edited by George H. Pollock, *How Psychiatrists Look at Aging* (New York: International Universities Press, 1992, 1994).

3. See Richard Friend, "Older Lesbian and Gay People: A Theory of Successful Aging," in *Gay Midlife and Maturity,* edited by John Allen Lee (New York: Harrington Press, 1990), p. 109.

4. See my earlier book, *Being Homosexual* (New York: Farrar, Straus & Giroux, 1989), pp. 82–93.

5. See Richard Steinman's report on his interviews with 280 women and men in relationships with young people, "Social Exchanges Between Older and Younger Gay Male Partners," in Lee, ed., *Gay Midlife and Maturity,* pp. 179–205.

6. Robert Stoller, "Blessed Denial: Or How, by Aging, I (Almost) Conquered Reality," in *How Psychiatrists Look at Aging,* edited by George H. Pollack, Vol. 1 (Madison, Conn.: International Universities Press, 1992), p. 227.

7. See Mary Jane Rotheram-Borus et al., "Predicting Patterns of Sexual Acts Among Homosexual and Bisexual Youths," *American Journal of Psychiatry* (1995), 152:4. More recently, James Driscoll, "AIDS Rising Again," Editorial, WashingtonTimes.com, December 12, 2007.

8. This issue is discussed by Walt Odets in his excellent and important article, "Why We Stopped Doing Primary Prevention for Gay Men in 1985," *AIDS and Public Policy Journal* (1995), 10(1):1–30.

9. Paul Monette, "The Politics of Silence," *The New York Times,* March 7, 1993.

Chapter 7: Opposing Institutional Bias: Antigay Discrimination in Psychoanalysis

1. Responding to an inquiry from Ernest Jones about accepting homosexuals for psychoanalytic training, Freud and Otto Rank wrote: "We do not on principle want to exclude such persons because we cannot condone their legal persecution. We believe that a decision in such cases should be reserved for an examination of the individual's other qualities." This letter was quoted in my earlier book, *Being Homosexual* (New York: Farrar, Straus & Giroux, 1989), p. 6. It was discovered by Dr. Hendric Ruitenbeck and is now in the Rare Books and Manuscript Library of Columbia University. It was first published in the Canadian gay newspaper *Body Politic* (1977), 33:8.

2. For a description of the disorders attributed to homosexuals by analysts over the past thirty years, see Kenneth Lewes, *The Psychoanalytic Theory of Male Homosexuality* (New York: Simon & Schuster, 1988), pp. 184–229.

3. D. J. West, *Homosexuality Re-Examined* (Minneapolis: University of Minnesota Press, 1977), p. 103.

4. See Ronald Bayer, *Homosexuality and American Psychiatry* (New York: Basic Books, 1981), pp. 121–42, for discussion of the APA's decision and the nature of the ensuing debate.

5. Ibid., p. 141.

6. Ibid., p. 121.

7. Otto Kernberg, "A Conceptual Model of Male Perversion," in *The Psychology of Men: New Psychoanalytic Perspectives,* edited by Gerald Fogel, Frederick Lane, and Robert Liebert (New York: Basic Books, 1986), p. 175.

8. Anna Freud, "Problems of Technique in Adult Analysis" (1954), in *The Writings of Anna Freud,* Vol. 4 (New York: International Universities Press, 1968), pp. 337–406. See also Lawrence Kolb and Adelaide Johnson, "Etiology and Therapy of Overt Homosexuality," *Psychoanalytic Quarterly* (1955), 24:506–16.

Similar admonitions were made by Lionel Ovesey and Sherwyn Wood, "Pseudohomosexuality and Homosexuality in Men: Psychodynamics as a Guide to Treatment," in *Homosexual Behavior*, edited by Judd Marmor (New York: Basic Books, 1980), pp. 325–41; and by Charles Socarides in *Homosexuality* (New York: Jason Aronson, 1978).

9. Selma Fraiberg, "Homosexual Conflicts," in *Adolescents: Psychoanalytic Approach to Problems and Therapy*, edited by S. Lozana and H. I. Schneer (New York: Paul E. Hober, 1961), p. 78. See also the description offered by my patient of the admonitions of his previous analyst, reported in *Being Homosexual*, p. 113.

10. In 1987 I asked a psychoanalyst who had done extensive research on patients accepted as low-fee cases for candidates in training about the prevailing attitude in his clinic toward treating homosexuals. He replied on February 4, 1987:

> This week the clinic committee evaluated a 42-year-old man. From the standpoint of your interest it is noteworthy that his homosexuality was not a subject of doubt as far as his acceptance was concerned. Ten years ago this man would undoubtedly have been turned down, partly for homosexuality and/or for his age. It is clear to me that he is accepted now, though conditionally, partly because the attitude for treating homosexual patients has changed and partly because the supply of good cases is sufficiently poor.

11. New views of adult masturbation as "normal" were presented at a meeting of the American Psychoanalytic Association in 1978. Even at the time, one highly regarded analyst took exception to "the modern views of our liberated society that adult masturbation is normal. . . . Contraceptive technology has contributed to a sex revolution that is tending to equalize masturbation and intercourse. . . . There is growing confusion between need satisfaction and mature psychological object-related fulfillment." Panel report, *Journal of the American Psychoanalytic Association* (1980), 28(3):647–48.

12. The report of the panel papers and the discussion that followed is summarized in *Journal of the American Psychoanalytic Association* (1984), op. cit.

13. Quoted in a letter dated February 16, 1984, from the editor of the *Journal of the American Psychoanalytic Association.*

14. Unpublished discussion of my paper, "Homosexuality in Homosexual and Heterosexual Men," presented at a meeting of the American Psychoanalytic Association, May 1985, Denver, Colorado. The paper was later published in *The Psychology of Men,* edited by Gerald Fogel, Frederick Lane, and Robert Liebert (New York: Basic Books, 1986).

15. Melvin Stanger, *PANY Bulletin* (1985):10–11.

16. Letter dated February 16, 1988, from the chairman of the Program Committee, summarizing reasons for the rejection of my paper on "Gay Men and Their Relationships."

17. "Whereas homosexuality per se implies no impairment in judgment, stability, reliability, or general social or vocational capabilities, therefore, be it resolved, that the American Psychiatric Association deplores all public and private discrimination against homosexuals in such areas as employment, housing, public accommodation, and licensing, and declares that no burden of proof of such judgment, capacity or reliability shall be placed upon homosexuals greater than that imposed on any other persons. Further, the American Psychiatric Association supports and urges the enactment of civil rights legislation at local, state and federal levels that would offer homosexual citizens the same protections now guaranteed to others. Further, the APA supports and urges the repeal of all discriminatory legislation singling out homosexual acts by consenting adults in private."

18. Article by Ken Hausman, *Psychiatric News,* July 21, 1989.

19. Letter from Homer C. Curtis, *Psychiatric News,* December 15, 1989, p. 50.

20. "American Academy Condemns Discrimination Against Gays," *Psychiatric News,* October 19, 1990.

21. "American Psychoanalytic Association Opposes Discrimination Against Homosexuals," *Psychiatric News,* August 2, 1991.

22. The statement on homosexuality adopted by the Executive Council on May 9, 1991, and amended April 30, 1992, stated:

> The American Psychoanalytic Association opposes and deplores public or private discrimination against male and female homosexually oriented individuals.
>
> It is the position of the American Psychoanalytic Association that our component institutes select candidates for training on the basis of their interest in psychoanalysis, talent, proper educational background, psychological integrity, analyzability and educability, and not on the basis of sexual orientation. It is expected that our component institutes will employ these standards for the selection of candidates for training and for the appointment of all grades of faculty including training and supervising analysts as well.

23. "American Psychoanalytic Association Goes a Step Further to Eliminate Bias Against Homosexual Applicants," *Psychiatric News,* July 17, 1992, p. 16.
24. Richard Isay, "Homosexuality and Psychiatry," *Psychiatric News,* February 7, 1992, p. 3.
25. The following notice was sent to psychoanalysts and other mental health professionals, along with the application to join NARTH:

> The National Association for Psychoanalytic Research and Therapy of Homosexuality was founded in March 1992 by psychoanalysts and psychoanalytically informed individuals who believe that homosexuality is a treatable developmental disorder. We have seen many homosexual men and women who are profoundly distressed by their condition. Homosexuality is completely contrary to their social and/or religious values and their conviction that all men and women are created naturally heterosexual.
>
> Our treatment methods are devised for those who voluntarily seek our help and who wish to search for the source of their disorder and its potential alleviation. There are many who do not wish to change their psychosexual adaptation, and we respect their wishes

not to seek change. We are also well aware that in certain types of homosexuality it is inadvisable to attempt extensive change.

This organization is being formed at this time to counter some disturbing recent movements within the psychiatric and psychological professions. The February 7, 1992 issue of *Psychiatric News,* published by the American Psychiatric Association, featured an article in the "From the President" column by Richard Isay, M.D., with an endorsement from APA President Lawrence Hartmann, M.D. This article contains two disturbing misstatements. The first implies that psychotherapists who treat homosexuals possess a malignant prejudice against these patients. The second states that if a clinician makes efforts "to change homosexuals to heterosexuals, this represents one of the most flagrant and frequent abuses of psychiatry in America."

Our aim is the healing and protection of those who in desperation seek our help. We want to be free to treat—with established psychoanalytic and psychotherapeutic methods—those patients who seek and are suitable for treatment.

We hope that the shared and published knowledge of how we work with patients will be an antidote to the current trend that accuses us of being "abusers of psychiatry." We are not a political organization, nor do we wish to diminish the rights of gay men and women in society.

26. Quoted in *American Psychoanalyst* (1993), 27(1):30.
27. Report of the Committee on Issues of Homosexuality, April 15, 1993.
28. Ralph Roughton, "Letter to the Editor," *American Psychoanalyst* (1992), 26(3). In response, see my letter *in American Psychoanalyst* (1993), 27(1):31.
29. Resolution passed by Executive Council, May 20, 1993.
30. Richard C. Friedman and Jennifer I. Downey, *Sexual Orientation and Psychodynamic Psychotherapy,* op. cit., p. 290.
31. Quoted in *NARTH Bulletin* (April 1995), 3(1):11.

Index